TWIST CHOCOLATE
VANILLA TWIST CHOC
TE VANILLA TWIST
CHOCOLATE VANILLA
IST CHOCOLATE VA
A TWIST CHOCOLA
NILLA TWIST CHOCO
VANILLA TWIST

# SWEET CREAM

## and

**90 RECIPES** FOR **MAKING YOUR OWN ICE CREAM** AND **FROZEN TREATS** FROM **BI-RITE CREAMERY**

# SUGAR CONES

### KRIS HOOGERHYDE,
### ANNE WALKER,
### and DABNEY GOUGH

## PHOTOGRAPHY BY PAIGE GREEN

TEN SPEED PRESS
BERKELEY

# CONTENTS

Mint Chip Ice Cream (page 182)

# INTRODUCTION

**MAKING THE ICE CREAM** wasn't the challenge. After all, we are pastry chefs, and producing ice cream, granitas, and sorbets had been part of our daily routine long before we opened our ice cream shop. We had the techniques down pat, and we knew what flavors worked well together. But in those early days before we opened the doors of Bi-Rite Creamery, the thing that worried us most was how we'd get enough people in the door.

There we were, sitting in one of the many planning meetings that took place before we opened, running the numbers to determine how many guests we would need each day in order to break even. When we realized that we would need to sell at least 150 ice cream cones on a given Saturday just to stay afloat, our stomachs sank. When you break it down, that comes out to *five cones every half hour.* It seemed a little unrealistic.

To our surprise and delight, it turned out not to be a problem. From the time we opened our doors on a typically cool and gray day in December 2006, there's been a near-constant line out the door. Our initial worry about how to get enough people in the door quickly changed to worrying about we could keep up with the demand.

Those 150 cones we set as the bare minimum? Within a few months of our grand opening we were selling that many within the first couple of hours each day; most Saturdays we sell ten times that, if not more. Last year we served more than half a million scoops of ice cream! It's kind of amazing, especially when you consider that every last scoop is made in a 100-square-foot state-certified room containing our one and only ice cream machine. With two full-time ice cream makers, Ezequiel and Luis, on staff, our machine hums from eight o'clock in the morning until five o'clock in the afternoon. On an average day, they pour fifty-one gallons of ice cream custard into the machine, enough to keep our case filled with eighteen to twenty different flavors, as well as fill our catering orders *and* the hand-pack containers for a handful of

local restaurants and our sister business, Bi-Rite Market.

It's hard to believe that owning an ice cream shop wasn't even part of our original plan. For about four years, we had been making cookies, cakes, pies, and other treats for sale at Bi-Rite Market. That whole time we had been working out of a rented commercial kitchen, and there came a point when it made more sense to get our own kitchen. We looked at a number of spots throughout the city and finally settled on a 700-square-foot space that had previously been an office on 18th Street in San Francisco's Mission District. The new spot was perfect: it was the right size, we could build the kitchen to our exact specifications, and it was just across the street from the Market where our goods were being sold.

It also featured a retail space—an unplanned-for bonus—though it took us a little while to decide what to do with it. With our baked goods already for sale at Bi-Rite Market, plus the extremely popular Tartine Bakery just down the street, it didn't make sense to open another

bakeshop. In the end, it was the space's proximity to Dolores Park that led us to open an ice cream shop. Every time we drove past the park while delivering our baked goods to the Market, we'd look at the park's hills dotted with people basking in the sun or playing with their kids. People who might want to come get a scoop of ice cream . . . or so we hoped!

Our hunch was right. In six years of being in business, Bi-Rite Creamery has become a destination for parkgoers, neighbors, and tourists alike, and it attracts a steady stream of guests—as many as two thousand on a warm Saturday. Our initial staff of four has grown to thirty scoopers, bakers, managers, dishwashers, and ice cream makers that we now include in our ever-growing family. We have been featured on the Food Network, in travel guides, and in the *New York Times,* and we have garnered more Yelp reviews than any other business in America.

## THE PURSUIT OF PURE FLAVOR

We are Anne Walker and Kris Hoogerhyde, founders of Bi-Rite Creamery. We started working together in 2000 at San Francisco's now-defunct 42 Degrees restaurant, where we made all of our ice cream by hand in an old-fashioned White Mountain ice cream machine that churned away on the restaurant's back patio.

During that period we became obsessed with making the most intensely flavored ice cream possible. We felt that all too often ice cream just didn't taste *enough* of whatever it was supposed to be. Sometimes we would even put a spoonful of ice cream in our mouths and have no idea what flavor we were eating. We believed that lemon ice cream should be really lemony. Butter pecan should taste like butter and pecans. Chocolate ice cream should be intensely chocolaty.

We wanted our ice cream to overwhelm your senses with flavor, so we constantly looked for ways to push the limits. This sometimes required

a lot of trial and error, but we kept at it until we got satisfactory results. By the time we opened our own shop we had already developed the recipes for many of the flavors we're best known for: honey lavender, brown butter pecan, roasted banana, and more.

Aside from the guidance we received from a few mentors over the years, we developed our recipes and figured out everything on our own. That's because the world of ice cream is shrouded in mystery: most ice cream pros keep their kitchens locked away from prying eyes and guard their recipes with their lives. Every aspect of making ice cream—from the techniques to the ingredients to the equipment itself—is usually treated as a trade secret.

We learned this the hard way when we were first starting out. While the Creamery was under construction and we were awaiting the delivery of our commercial machine, we used home-kitchen ice cream machines to fine-tune our recipes. Our commercial ice cream machine didn't arrive until a week before we were set to open. When we opened the crate we realized that the instruction manual didn't give many specifics, and it certainly didn't answer all the questions that we had. After calling the manufacturer and searching online, we still didn't understand the finer points of running the machine: how to fine-tune the controls, how long to freeze a batch of ice cream, or the best way to maintain it. We asked local owners of the same model for advice and, much to our surprise, they all turned us down! Some of these people were (and still are) close friends of ours, but they were firm in their refusal. It's not like we were asking for their recipes; we just wanted tips on adjusting and maintaining the machine! But even that information was considered a secret. We eventually worked out the details on our own, but that experience taught us a lot about the idiosyncrasies of the ice cream business.

Our approach is different. When we built our space, we situated our ice cream making room behind a huge window that faced 18th Street, putting our ice cream machine in full view of anyone who happened to walk by the shop. Our kitchen was similarly open; since it was located next to the front counter, visitors might see a batch of roasted bananas coming out of the oven, trays of cookies cooling on a rack, or sugar caramelizing on one of the six stovetop burners.

We've since expanded and remodeled, so the setup has changed a bit since those early days. However, our secret is still in plain sight: *we make everything by hand and in small batches, in a regular kitchen using real, fresh ingredients.*

It's a simple approach, but it makes all the difference. Our dairy products come from Straus Family Creamery, the first certified organic dairy west of the Mississippi. Their small herd grazes on the rolling hills overlooking Tomales Bay in Marin County, only thirty miles away. The cows are healthy and happy and produce milk that is rich and flavorful, which makes it the perfect neutral background for our ice creams.

We also use organic sugar and eggs, obtaining them locally whenever possible. In fact, although we buy in large quantities from our suppliers, they're the same ingredients that you might find at the grocery store.

We make our ice cream in small batches, which gives us greater control over the quality of each and every scoop. It also helps us maintain a tight inventory with high turnover. That means that when you come into our shop, the ice creams in the case were made within the past few days. And, although most people don't realize it, an ice cream's freshness really matters. If it is stored for too long, an ice cream's flavors become muted and dull.

We don't skimp on ingredients, either. We use real vanilla beans from Madagascar for a more complex, heady vanilla taste and aroma. For our coffee ice cream, we start with freshly ground beans from our neighbors at Ritual Coffee Roasters, who roast and brew some of the best coffee in the country. We special order our macadamia nuts from Mahina Mele Farm in Hawaii because they're the most buttery, crunchy macadamia nuts we've ever tasted.

We also support local farms and respect the seasons. Balsamic Strawberry (page 138) is one of our most popular flavors, but we only make it in the spring and summer, when local strawberries are at their juicy, fragrant peak. We get our strawberries (specifically, the super-sweet but delicate Chandler variety) from a handful of nearby farms. We source all of our fruit through the buyers at our sister business, Bi-Rite Market, which is known far and wide for its incredible farm-direct produce.

And when we say our ice cream is "hand-made," we really mean it. We make nearly everything that we fold into our ice cream, from the marshmallows in our Rocky Road to the almond toffee pieces that give our Coffee Toffee its crunch. Sure, we could just buy mini-marshmallows and toffee bars instead of making them ourselves, but the end product wouldn't taste nearly as good.

The result of all this is ice cream that is rich, intense, and unmistakably Bi-Rite.

## WHY WE WROTE THIS BOOK: THE IMPORTANCE OF SHARING

We get so much out of making and sharing a product that makes people smile. And, with the cultlike following that we've developed, it might seem strange that we'd give away our recipes in the form of a cookbook.

One of the best pastry chefs Anne ever worked for gave away every recipe. There's something beautiful about sharing knowledge and encouraging others to learn and develop new skills.

And we love cookbooks. It's so exciting to discover a book full of recipes that you want to make, and to find that all of the recipes really work. To open up the book and get a straightforward understanding of how ingredients work together.

There's something really fun about making ice cream. When you make ice cream at home, you're probably not making it just for yourself. You're making it to share. A freshly churned

batch is reason enough to come together, scoop out a few bowls, and enjoy an afternoon with friends or family.

Making your own ice cream also enables you to tweak the recipe to your taste, to invent your own flavors, and to add your own little touches. When you make it yourself, you know you're getting a really good product, just the way you like it.

Even if you've never visited Bi-Rite Creamery, and even if you've never made your own ice cream, we hope that this book will inspire you to create delicious treats and share them with your friends and family.

# BASIC INGREDIENTS *and* EQUIPMENT

USING GOOD INGREDIENTS is key to making delicious ice cream, and having the right equipment will make your life much easier!

## INGREDIENTS

As you flip through this book, you may notice that we call for relatively few ingredients in each recipe. Moreover, the same simple items appear over and over: eggs, cream, milk, sugar, and salt. There are no "secret ingredients" in our recipes; rather, we use the best-quality ingredients we can find. That means buying organic milk and cream from a local dairy and spending a little extra on organic sugar, among other things. Really *good* ingredients are what makes our ice cream taste so good.

### EGGS

We always call for large eggs in our recipes, simply because doing so produces more consistent results. Within a carton of a dozen large eggs, you will find that the yolks vary in size, but using large eggs still provides sufficient uniformity.

We prefer to use organic eggs, because doing so ensures that the eggs come from chickens that have access to the outdoors, eat organic feed, and are raised without the use of preventative antibiotics. If available, pastured eggs are our eggs of choice, since they have much more flavor than commercial eggs. Pastured eggs come from chickens that live in an open pasture, where they are able to forage a natural diet of bugs, worms, and grasses. (Regular commercial eggs come from chickens that live indoors in cramped conditions and are fed a diet consisting primarily of corn, soy, and, unless vegetarian feed is specified, poultry by-products plus a cocktail of antibiotics.)

Our ice cream recipes call for egg yolks, which means you'll need to separate the yolks from the whites. Cold eggs are easier to separate than ones at room temperature, so separate them as soon as you take them out of the refrigerator.

You'll need two bowls, one for the yolks and one for the whites. Use one of the two following techniques:

**The conventional way:** Crack the egg sharply on the counter and, holding the egg over a bowl, carefully break open the shell without letting the egg fall out. Gently pass the egg back and forth between the two shell halves until the white has slipped out into the bowl below. Drop the yolk into the second bowl.

**The pro way:** Cup your hand and hold it over one of the bowls. With the other hand, crack the egg sharply on the counter. Empty the egg into your cupped hand, allowing the white to slip through your fingers and into the bowl below. Drop the yolk into the second bowl.

> **TIP:** *What should you do with all those leftover egg whites? You could always make Meringue (page 50) or Marshmallows (page 52), throw them into your breakfast scramble, or use them in cocktail recipes that call for an egg white. But don't feel rushed to use them up. If refrigerated, the whites will stay good for at least a couple of weeks.*

### HEAVY CREAM AND MILK

We get our dairy products from Straus Family Creamery, which is located just north of us in Marin County. This small, family-owned business was the first certified organic dairy west of the Mississippi, and they produce some of the best-tasting milk and cream we've ever had. Wherever you live, seek out organic milk and cream from a local dairy. It supports your local community and is better for the cow and the environment.

Almost all of our ice cream recipes call for a combination of heavy cream and low-fat milk. Why not just heavy cream? Too much fat can mask the other flavors in ice cream and it weighs heavy on the tongue. Cream that is cut with a little 1 percent or 2 percent milk provides the perfect balance of richness and flavor.

> **TIP:** *Heavy cream is sometimes labeled "heavy whipping cream." Cream labeled "whipping cream" (but without the word "heavy") has a slightly lower fat content, but it will still work fine in our recipes.*

### SUGAR

Once upon a time, **granulated sugar** came from only one source: sugarcane. But over the years, some producers have switched to using genetically modified (GM) sugar beets to make sugar because it is more profitable. At the Creamery, not only do we avoid GM foods and products as a rule, but we avoid beet sugar simply because it does not perform as well in many baking and pastry applications. So make sure the package says "pure cane sugar."

For environmental and health reasons, we use organic sugar at the Creamery. With just a few exceptions, it measures and cooks the same as nonorganic sugar, and, with its tiny hint of molasses flavor, it is truer to what sugarcane really tastes like. However, organic sugar can behave temperamentally in recipes involving caramelization, like our Salted Caramel Ice Cream (page 61) or Bananas Brûlée (page 207). This is because organic sugar is slightly less refined and contains tiny particles that are prone to burning when the sugar is cooked on its own. So for the home cook making caramel, conventional (nonorganic) white cane sugar is more foolproof.

For recipes that call for **brown sugar**, you can use light or dark brown sugar (or a combination) with equal success. Dark brown sugar has a more assertive, robust flavor that can mask delicate flavors, so if you use it, make sure that the other ingredients in the recipe will stand up to it. Light brown sugar plays well with nearly any ingredients. When you measure brown sugar, be sure to pack it firmly into the measuring cup.

**Powdered sugar** (also known as confectioners' sugar) has been milled to a very fine consistency and mixed with a small amount of cornstarch to prevent clumping. Always measure it first, then sift it to remove any clumps.

**Turbinado sugar** has a golden hue, coarse texture, and does not melt when baked. We use it to coat balls of cookie dough before they go into the oven to give the cookies a bit of sparkle and a pleasant crunch. You can use regular granulated sugar instead of turbinado, but you won't get the same texture or color.

### SALT

Even in desserts, a tiny bit of salt helps to amplify flavors, and in some cases salt plays an important chemical role. We use kosher salt for all of our recipes.

### FLOUR

We use unbleached, organic all-purpose flour for all of our baking recipes. If you can find it, stone-ground flour offers better flavor and texture and more nutrients compared to the more common roller-milled type.

### TAPIOCA SYRUP

Many baking, confectionary, and sorbet recipes rely on corn syrup to lend a sticky, viscous quality to the end product—pecan pie is a great example of what corn syrup can do. But conventional corn syrup is made from genetically modified corn, which we avoid. There are organic versions of corn syrup, but they are much runnier and do not produce the same results. We've found that organic tapioca syrup is a perfect stand-in for corn syrup and can be substituted in an equal amount. See Sources (page 210) for more info.

## EQUIPMENT

Yes, you do need an ice cream machine to make ice cream, but aside from that you probably already have (or can improvise) just about everything else you need. Here is a rundown of tools that are used again and again in our recipes.

### ICE CREAM MACHINE

You don't need a fancy ice cream machine; all of the recipes in this book were tested using a standard household machine with a freezable mixing bowl. This basic, inexpensive variety will work just fine for most people's needs. The only drawbacks are that you have to have the foresight to freeze the bowl before you need it (or devote the freezer space to give it a permanent home there), and you must refreeze the bowl completely between each use. Depending on your freezer temperature, it can take anywhere from ten to eighteen hours for the bowl to freeze solid. Cuisinart makes a great ice cream maker; KitchenAid makes a bowl that fits into their stand mixer, which is nice because it keeps you from having to store an extra piece of equipment.

If you see lots of ice cream in your future, you can invest in a high-end model with a built-in cooling unit. This type of machine lets you make ice cream on the fly (without prefreezing a mixing bowl) and also allows you to make multiple batches back to back. They are, however, more expensive, heavier, and take up a lot more space.

If you want to go old-school, you can certainly use an old-fashioned ice-and-rock salt machine, like the ones made by White Mountain. They work great, and the nostalgia factor is undeniable. This is the type of machine we used for years at 42 Degrees and it always produced a wonderful product. These machines typically have a much larger capacity than electric models, so you'll need to scale up our recipes for the best results. (A single quart of base spinning in a 4-quart machine won't churn properly.)

Whatever type of machine you use, make sure it has a capacity of at least 1½ quarts. Although most of our recipes make about 1 quart of finished ice cream, you need the extra space for the ice cream to churn around in.

FOR ICE CREAM, YOU'LL ALSO NEED . . .

- **A medium heatproof bowl** for the egg yolks.

- **A 2-cup heatproof liquid measuring cup** for the cream and milk.

- **A medium nonreactive saucepan.** Don't use unlined aluminum, which is reactive and can cause foods that come in direct contact with it to discolor. A heavy pan will distribute heat evenly—useful for all cooking, but especially important when making caramel. We generally call for small (2-quart) and medium (3- to 4-quart) saucepans. Although it's not necessary to use pans precisely that size, for the best results you should try to stay within a quart or so of the size indicated.

- **A heatproof rubber spatula** for stirring the base as it cooks (better than a spoon because it has more contact with the bottom of the pan).

- **A wooden spoon** (optional) for testing the progress of the base as it thickens.

- **A ladle** for tempering the eggs.

- **Dry measuring cups** for sugar and other dry ingredients.

- **Measuring spoons** for salt, vanilla extract, and other ingredients.

- **A fine-mesh strainer** set over a heatproof container (a 4-cup Pyrex measuring cup is the perfect size and will be fairly stable in the ice-water bath).

- **A whisk** for mixing and tempering the eggs.

- **A large bowl** for the ice-water bath.

YOU MAY ALSO NEED . . .

- **A blender or food processor** for grinding nuts and puréeing fruits and other mixtures.

- **A digital scale** to weigh your flour. The easiest way to improve your baking is to use a scale instead of dry measuring cups. You'll get much more accurate, consistent results. Plus you can measure items directly into the mixing bowl, which means no measuring cups to clean!

- **A stand mixer** for mixing cookie doughs and cake batters and whipping egg whites and frostings. Handheld mixers will work for liquidy mixtures such as meringues, but they are not sturdy enough to handle stiff things like cookie dough.

- **Pop molds.** Most have a capacity of 3 ounces per pop. If you don't want to invest in a pop mold, you can use 3-ounce waxed paper cups instead.

- **Rimmed baking sheets.** Heavy commercial ones are the best; they conduct heat evenly, are more durable, and are less prone to warping. For home use, "half"-size baking sheets (13 by 18 inches) are perfect.

- **Nonstick baking mats,** which are commonly sold under the brand name Silpat. These reusable mats eliminate the need for parchment paper. They are not only great for cookies but also work perfectly for the peanut brittle and almond toffee recipes.

- **A rasp-style grater,** often sold under the Microplane brand, that produces fine, wispy threads of whatever you're grating. It is especially good for zesting citrus, since the shallow blades cut only as deep as the flavorful zest and leave the bitter pith behind.

- **A small metal offset spatula** (with a blade about 4 inches long) for smoothing the tops of ice cream cakes and spreading glaze evenly.

- **A propane or butane kitchen torch** for toasting meringue or caramelizing bananas for your banana split. It's also handy when slicing an ice cream cake or pie; instead of dipping your knife into a glass of hot water, you can just wave the flame over the blade to heat it up. You might not use it every day, but you'll be glad you have it when you need it.

- **A candy thermometer,** which is essential for making candy such as Marshmallows (page 52), Almond Toffee (page 68), and Peanut Brittle (page 131). We like to use one made by Taylor that is readily available in kitchen supply stores.

- **A double boiler,** for gently melting chocolate and heating mixtures containing eggs. You can create your own double boiler by setting a nonreactive bowl over a saucepan with gently simmering water. Use a pan that is wide enough to comfrotably hold the bowl, and make sure the bottom of the bowl does not come into contact with the water. If you have a gas stove, make sure the flame does not reach up the sides of the saucepan or bowl.

# TECHNIQUES

FOR THOSE WHO are making ice cream, sorbet, or other frozen treats for the first time, these master instructions provide a detailed, step-by-step guide for what to do, when, and why.

## ICE CREAM MASTER INSTRUCTIONS

The instructions given here are for a basic ice cream. Recipes in this book may have additional or modified steps, depending on the flavor.

TOOLS

- Liquid and dry measuring cups
- Measuring spoons
- Medium heatproof bowl
- Whisk
- Medium (3- or 4-quart) nonreactive saucepan
- Wooden spoon (optional)
- Ladle
- Heatproof rubber spatula
- Fine-mesh strainer
- Another heatproof bowl or other container for the cooked base (see Tip)
- A large bowl of ice water (big enough to comfortably hold the container of cooked base)
- Ice cream machine with at least a 1½-quart capacity

TIP: *The container filled with the cooked base will end up sitting in a bath of ice water to speed cooling. A large (4-cup) Pyrex measuring cup works particularly well, as the flat bottom and the extra weight of the glass keep it from bobbing around in the water.*

BASIC INGREDIENTS

- Egg yolks
- Sugar
- 1% or 2% milk
- Heavy cream
- Kosher salt

Step 1

Step 3

Step 5

## GET READY

Gather all necessary equipment and set out and measure all your ingredients. In a large bowl, make an ice water bath.

## MAKE THE BASE

1.  Put the egg yolks in a medium heatproof bowl and whisk just long enough to break them up. Add half of the sugar and whisk just until blended. Set aside. (Adding some of the sugar to the eggs dilutes them a bit and helps prevent them from scrambling when you add the hot cream.)

2.  In a medium nonreactive saucepan, stir together the milk, cream, the remaining half of the sugar, and the salt. (Heating the rest of the sugar with the cream helps it dissolve faster.)

3.  Put the pan over medium-high heat. Stir occasionally and watch closely as the cream heats up (it can boil over easily). You want to bring it just to the brink of simmering. A few things will happen that will tell you you're getting close: bubbles will form and break along the edge of the pan, and then you'll notice that the mixture will seem to swell slightly.

4.  When the mixture approaches a simmer, reduce the heat to medium. (It's not the end of the world if it does come to a simmer or even a boil at this point, but it's not necessary.)

5.  With a measuring cup or a ladle, carefully scoop out about ½ cup of the hot cream mixture and, whisking the eggs constantly, add the cream to the bowl with the egg yolks. Repeat, adding another ½ cup of the

Step 6

Step 7

Step 8

hot cream to the bowl with the egg yolks. The purpose of this step is to gently heat the egg yolks (also known as "tempering" them), which reduces the risk of overcooking them.

6. Return your attention to the saucepan. Using a heatproof rubber spatula or wooden spoon, stir the cream as you slowly pour the cream-and-egg-yolk mixture from the bowl into the pan. Continue to cook on medium heat, stirring constantly with the spatula in a figure-eight pattern to make sure that you're covering the entire bottom of the pan.

**TIP:** *Now that the egg yolks are in the saucepan, you need to keep the heat low and gentle; otherwise the eggs will scramble and your base will "break." So if you're new to ice cream making, reduce the heat to low to slow the process down and make it easier to observe. (It will, of course, take a little longer this way.)*

Pay close attention to the consistency as the base cooks, as it can change quickly and dramatically. Your goal is to have it go from the consistency of heavy cream to that of a thinnish puréed soup, *but no thicker.* You'll notice that the mixture will start to thicken slightly and you'll feel a little more resistance as you stir.

7. Test the readiness by removing the spatula from the saucepan and dragging your finger across it. If the base coats the back of the spatula, and the path created by your finger holds for a second or two (that is, the base doesn't immediately start running down the side of the spatula), it's ready. You can also try this test using a wooden spoon. It can be easier to judge the doneness of a light-colored base against the dark background of a wooden spoon.

**TIP:** *After adding the egg yolk mixture to the saucepan, it might take anywhere from 1 to 5 minutes for the base to thicken properly. The amount of time depends on your stove, the size and shape of the pan you're using, and how hot the cream mixture was to start with. Be patient and pay close attention as it cooks—practice is the best teacher!*

Step 9

8. As soon as the base has reached the correct consistency, remove the pan from the heat and immediately pour the base through the fine-mesh strainer and into a clean bowl or large Pyrex measuring cup. The base will continue to cook and thicken in the pan even after it has been removed from the burner, which is why it's important to act quickly once it reaches the right consistency. Now wash your spatula.

**TIP:** *If you overcook or "break" the ice cream base, you can bring it back to life by puréeing it with an immersion blender (a regular blender will work fine as well). This will smooth out the texture and emulsify the mixture. Then strain and chill the base as directed.*

**TIP:** *The spatula may have traces of uncooked eggs on it, so washing it now is an important step to prevent potential foodborne illness.*

## CHILL THE BASE

9. Set the bowl or measuring cup containing the base into the ice-water bath and stir frequently with the clean spatula until cool. Remove from the ice-water bath, cover with plastic wrap, and chill the mixture until completely cold, at least 2 hours but ideally overnight.

Step 10

## FREEZE THE ICE CREAM

**10.** Once the base is thoroughly chilled, freeze it in your ice cream machine according to the manufacturer's instructions.

**TIP:** *While the ice cream is churning, put the storage container into the freezer. This will keep the ice cream from melting as you transfer it.*

How will you know when it's ready? You should stop churning when the ice cream reaches the consistency of soft-serve ice cream, or once it has a smooth consistency and the paddles creates a distinct path in its wake. (See the photo on page 15 for an example.) The exact timing varies from one machine to the next. It will firm up in the freezer. In any case, be careful not to overchurn the ice cream, which can cause the butterfat to separate out, producing an unpleasant texture. There is no way to fix an overchurned ice cream, so be careful to keep an eye on it as it approaches the finished stage.

If you're using any mix-ins like chopped nuts or grated chocolate, add them in the last minute or so of churning, or fold them in by hand once you turn off the machine. (Work quickly so that the ice cream doesn't melt!)

**11.** Enjoy the ice cream right away, or transfer it to a chilled storage container and store it in the freezer for up to a week. Any longer than that and the flavors will start to diminish.

**TIP:** *Freezing churned ice cream prior to serving it allows the ice cream to firm up and further develop its flavors. The colder your freezer, the better.*

# SORBET MASTER INSTRUCTIONS

The instructions given here are for a basic sorbet. Recipes in this book may have additional or modified steps, depending on the flavor.

For the best results, make sorbet the same day you plan to serve it; otherwise, it can become very hard and icy.

## TOOLS

- Liquid and dry measuring cups
- Measuring spoons
- Spoon
- Medium bowl
- Ice cream machine with at least a 1½-quart capacity

## BASIC INGREDIENTS

- Fruit juice, as specified in the recipe
- Prepared and cooled simple syrup (page 18) or sugar
- Kosher salt

## MAKE THE BASE

1. Combine all of the ingredients in a bowl and stir well to blend. Make sure the salt is completely dissolved.

   **TIP:** *Even within a single variety of fruit, you'll find different levels of sweetness depending on where the fruit was grown and when it was harvested; you may need to adjust the amount of simple syrup. Add a little less syrup to start, taste, and add more syrup if necessary. The sorbet will seem less sweet once frozen, so the liquid base should taste slightly too sweet.*

## FREEZE THE SORBET

2. Freeze in your ice cream machine according to the manufacturer's instructions. You'll know it's ready when it gets lighter in color and goes from a slushy consistency to a smoother, firmer one. Sorbet takes longer to freeze than ice cream, and, unlike ice cream, there's no danger of overchurning it.

   **TIP:** *While the sorbet is churning, put the container you'll use to store it into the freezer. This will prevent the sorbet from melting as you transfer it.*

3. Enjoy right away, or transfer the sorbet to the chilled storage container. For a firmer sorbet, freeze for about 4 hours.

   **TIP:** *To easily scoop hardened sorbet, let it sit out at room temperature for 10 minutes. Dip your scoop in warm water and pat dry between each scoop.*

## 1:1 SIMPLE SYRUP

Simple syrup can be stored in your fridge nearly indefinitely. You can use it to make homemade lemonade, sweeten iced coffee, or make a sorbet. It is always nice to have on hand, so double or triple the batch if you like.

1/2 cup sugar
1/2 cup water

1. Mix the sugar and water in a small saucepan. Dip your fingers or a pastry brush in water and wash down the sides of the pan before heating (stray sugar crystals can prevent the syrup from melting properly).
2. Place over medium heat and stir until the mixture comes to a boil and the sugar has dissolved completely.
3. Remove the pan from the heat and let cool completely. Transfer to a covered container and store in the refrigerator.

## 2:1 SIMPLE SYRUP

This simple syrup has twice as much sugar than it does water, making it more viscous. We use it in pops when the fruit juice is already fairly watery.

1/2 cup sugar
1/4 cup water

1. Mix the sugar and water in a small saucepan. Dip your fingers or a pastry brush in water and wash down the sides of the pan before heating (stray sugar crystals can prevent the syrup from melting properly).
2. Place over medium heat and stir until the mixture comes to a boil and the sugar has dissolved completely.
3. Remove the pan from the heat and let cool completely. Transfer to a covered container and store in the refrigerator.

# GRANITA MASTER INSTRUCTIONS

Be sure to budget plenty of time for a granita to freeze. It can take 3 hours or longer, depending on the size and shape of the container and the temperature of your freezer.

The instructions given here are for a basic granita. Recipes in this book may have additional or modified steps, depending on the flavor.

For the best results, make the granita the same day you plan to serve it; otherwise, you may need to let it soften slightly and scrape it again to obtain that light, feathery texture.

TOOLS

- Liquid and dry measuring cups
- Measuring spoons
- Spoon
- Medium bowl
- 8- or 9-inch square baking dish, or a similar shallow dish
- Fork

Step 2

Step 3

## BASIC INGREDIENTS

- Prepared and cooled simple syrup (page 18) or sugar
- Fruit juice or other flavorful liquid, as specified in the recipe
- Kosher salt

## MAKE THE BASE

1. Combine all of the ingredients in a bowl and stir well to blend. Make sure the salt is completely dissolved.

   **TIP:** *Even within a single variety of fruit, you'll find different levels of sweetness depending on where the fruit was grown and when it was harvested. For that reason, you may need to use more or less simple syrup depending on the sweetness of the fruit. To be safe, you can add a little less syrup to start, taste, and add more syrup if necessary. The granita will seem less sweet once frozen, so the liquid base should taste slightly too sweet.*

## FREEZE THE GRANITA

2. Pour the mixture into an 8- or 9-inch square baking dish or similar shallow dish. Freeze uncovered for 1 hour, or until ice crystals start to form.
3. Stir the mixture with a fork to break up the crystals. Return the baking dish to the freezer and stir every 30 minutes or so to break up the ice crystals as the granita freezes. When the granita is completely frozen (2½ to 3 hours total) it should have a light, feathery texture.
4. Serve right away or transfer to a resealable container and store in the freezer. If stored, break up the mixture with a fork just before serving.

# ICE POPS MASTER INSTRUCTIONS

The instructions given here are for basic pops. Recipes in this book may have additional or modified steps, depending on the flavor.

## TOOLS

- Liquid and dry measuring cups
- Medium bowl
- Spoon
- Fine-mesh strainer (optional)
- Ice pop molds or 3-ounce waxed paper cups
- Ice pop sticks

## BASIC INGREDIENTS

- Fruit juice, as specified in the recipe
- Prepared and cooled simple syrup (page 18) or sugar
- Kosher salt

## MAKE THE BASE

1. Combine all of the ingredients in a bowl and stir well to blend. Make sure the salt is completely dissolved. Taste and add more simple syrup as needed.

    **TIP:** *Even within a single variety of fruit, you'll find different levels of sweetness depending on where the fruit was grown and when it was harvested. For that reason, when making juice-based pops, you may need to use more or less simple syrup depending on the sweetness of the fruit. To be safe, you can add a little less syrup to start, taste, and add more syrup if necessary. The pops will seem less sweet once frozen, so the liquid base should taste slightly too sweet.*

2. If desired, strain the base through a fine-mesh strainer.

    **TIP:** *Straining the base produces a smoother (but often icier) consistency. Skip this step if you want your pops to have a little more texture.*

## FREEZE THE POPS

3. Transfer the base to a liquid measuring cup. Pour the base into ice pop molds or cups, dividing it evenly, and insert the sticks. (If using cups, you'll need to let the base partially freeze before inserting the sticks.)
4. Freeze until completely solid, about 4 hours.
5. Unmold just before serving. If using molds, invert and run under hot tap water just until the pops release. If using paper cups, peel the cups away from the pops.

# ICE CREAM CAKE ASSEMBLY

Our ice cream cakes are about two parts ice cream to one part cake, which we think is the optimal ratio.

The easiest way to make an ice cream cake is to have the baked, trimmed cake base in the pan and ready to go before you churn your ice cream. That way you can transfer the ice cream directly from the machine onto the cake base. If your ice cream is already frozen, however, you can certainly use it; you'll just need to soften it in the refrigerator and mix it in a stand mixer to get it to the optimal spreading consistency. (See page 22, step 5.)

## TOOLS

- 8-inch diameter by 3-inches deep round cake pan or an 8-inch springform pan

- Parchment or waxed paper

- Scissors

- A serrated knife

- A pastry brush, if topping the cake base with a sauce or syrup

- A stand mixer with the paddle attachment, if using already-frozen ice cream

- A rubber spatula

- A metal offset spatula

- Aluminum foil, if using a springform pan

- Two plates at least as big as the cake (one for transferring, one for serving), or one plate and one 8-inch round of cardboard

## INGREDIENTS

- Nonstick cooking spray, or butter or oil

- A single 8-inch round layer of cake, baked and cooled completely (see page 24 for suggestions)

- About ½ cup inclusions such as nuts, chopped candies, sauce, or cookie pieces for the cake base (optional; see page 24 for suggestions)

- 2 quarts (2 batches) ice cream

- Cake decorations of your choice (optional; see page 24 for suggestions)

- Frosting, glaze, or meringue of your choice

## TIMELINE

This timeline assumes that your ice cream machine will accommodate a double batch (about 2 quarts) of ice cream. If your machine has a smaller capacity, you'll need to freeze the ice cream in two batches. Additionally, if your machine uses a bowl that you prefreeze before churning, be sure to allow an extra day in the timeline to refreeze the bowl between batches.

- **Two days before:** Make a double batch of ice cream base and chill.

- **One day before:** Bake the cake and cool completely. Prepare the cake base and the pan. Churn the ice cream base in your machine and transfer directly to the prepared pan. Freeze.

- **The morning of:** Unmold the cake, decorate, and freeze until ready to serve.

- **5 minutes before:** Let the cake sit at room temperature before slicing.

## METHOD

1. **Prepare the cake pan.** Spray a cake pan that's 8 inches in diameter and at least 3 inches deep with nonstick cooking spray. (You can also use a springform pan of the same dimensions. Wrap the outside bottom and sides of the pan tightly with aluminum foil to prevent water from seeping in during the unmolding step.)

2. **Line the pan with parchment paper.** This will make it easier to get the finished cake out of the pan. Line the bottom of the cake pan with a circle of parchment or waxed paper. Then cut two strips of parchment that are 3 inches wide by 14 inches long. Line the sides of the pan with the parchment strips, overlapping them slightly. Spray a bit of non-stick spray (or dot with butter or mist with oil) where the ends overlap to help them adhere.

Step 2

Step 4

Step 5

**SWEET CREAM** *and* **SUGAR CONES**

Step 5, continued

**TIP:** *If you're using a sauce that has been refrigerated, rewarm it gently by microwaving it at half power for 1 to 2 minutes, or place the container in a pan of gently simmering water, stirring frequently until the sauce becomes more fluid.*

5. **Top with ice cream.** If you have just-churned, soft ice cream, transfer it directly from the machine into the cake pan.

   If your ice cream has been stored in the freezer, allow it to soften in the refrigerator for 20 to 30 minutes; at the same time, put the bowl of your stand mixer, the paddle attachment, and the cake and pan in the freezer to chill while the ice cream softens. When it's slightly softened, put the ice cream in the mixer bowl and beat on low speed just until the ice cream is malleable, about 30 seconds. (It doesn't need to be completely smooth, just spreadable.) Transfer the ice cream to the cake pan.

   Use the offset spatula to nudge the ice cream all the way to the sides of the pan, filling any gaps or holes, including any space between the cake and the pan. Rap the filled cake pan sharply on the counter a few times to encourage any air bubbles to rise to the surface and smooth the top. If adding any candies or nuts, sprinkle these onto the surface of the ice cream before freezing.

   Put the assembled cake in the freezer as soon as it's filled and freeze overnight.

**TIP:** *If you like, you can use two different flavors of ice cream. You'll need 1 quart of each flavor, and you'll get the best results by building the layers in stages. Add the first layer of ice cream to the prepared cake base, freeze for a few hours to solidify, then add the second layer of ice cream. Freeze the completed cake overnight as you would a single-flavor cake.*

3. **Prepare the cake base.** You will need a 1 inch high layer of cake for the base of your ice cream cake. To achieve this, take an 8-inch baked cake, place it on a flat work surface, and trim off the domed top portion with a long serrated knife to achieve a level surface. If the cake is more than 2 inches high, split it horizontally to achieve two layers. Place one of the layers in the bottom of the prepared cake pan for the base of your ice cream cake and wrap and freeze the remaining layer for another cake.

4. **Brush, drizzle, or sprinkle the inclusions of your choice over the cake base (optional).** Distribute it as evenly as possible.

**TIP:** *For ice creams that contain swirled-in sauces (like the Peanut Butter Fudge Swirl on page 123), too much stirring or manipulation, including the process of building the ice cream cake, can produce muddy-looking results. If you want to use one of these flavors in an ice cream cake, just freeze the ice cream base as instructed by the recipe and incorporate the swirl once the ice cream is in the prepared cake pan.*

6. **At least 1 hour (and no more than 12 hours) before serving, unmold the cake.** To release the cake from the pan, invert the cake onto a plate or cardboard round the same size or *smaller* than the cake pan and run the pan under warm tap water until the cake loosens. (If you are using a springform pan, be sure to wrap the seams tightly in aluminum foil before running under the warm water to prevent water from leaking into in the cake and ice cream.) Remove the parchment. Top with a serving plate (or 8-inch round of cardboard) and turn the cake right side up.

7. **Decorate with the toppings (frostings, glazes, meringue, or whipped cream) of your choice,** working quickly so that the ice cream doesn't melt, and freeze until ready to serve. Or put the undecorated cake back in the freezer and decorate closer to serving time. Covered with foil, the cake will keep in the freezer for 2 days.

8. **Serve the cake.** Remove the cake from the freezer 5 minutes before serving to soften it slightly. A hot, dry knife will yield the cleanest cuts. Dip your knife in a glass of hot water, wipe it clean with a towel, and cut a slice. Repeat between every slice.

## OUR FAVORITE ICE CREAM CAKE COMBOS

*Mint Chip (shown on page 173)*
Mint Chip Ice Cream (page 182)
Chocolate Midnight Cake (page 88)
Chocolate Glaze (page 94)
Chocolate Shavings (page 97)

*Coffee Toffee (shown on page 102)*
Coffee Toffee Ice Cream (see Coffee Ice Cream note, page 104)
Chocolate Midnight Cake (page 88)
Chopped Almond Toffee (page 68)

*Balsamic Strawberry "Shortcake" (shown on page 139)*
Balsamic Strawberry Ice Cream (page 138)
Great Yellow Cake (page 42)
Whipped Cream (page 51)
Sliced Strawberry Topping (page 149)

*Pumpkin Spice (shown on page 194)*
Pumpkin Pie Ice Cream (page 185)
Evadne's Gingerbread (page 193)
Caramel Sauce (page 71)
Spiced Pecans (page 132)

---

**MAKE IT YOUR OWN**

✳ Create your own ice cream cake by choosing a cake base, one or two ice cream flavors, and one or more toppings.

A food processor is ideal for making fine, even crumbs for this crust.

...........................................

1¹/₂ cups fine cookie crumbs, from homemade or
    storebought cookies
2 tablespoons sugar
2 tablespoons unsalted butter, melted
Pinch of kosher salt

1. Position a rack in the center of the oven and preheat the oven to 350°F.
2. In a small bowl, combine all of the ingredients until evenly blended. The mixture will be crumbly but should hold together when you pinch some between your fingers. Transfer to a 9-inch pie pan and distribute evenly along the bottom and sides of the pan. Use a drinking glass or other flat-bottomed object to press the crumbs to an even thickness.
3. Bake until the crust is light golden brown, 8 to 10 minutes. Remove from the oven and let cool completely.

# ICE CREAM PIE ASSEMBLY

The easiest way to make an ice cream pie is to have the baked, cooled piecrust ready to go before you churn your ice cream. That way you can transfer the finished ice cream directly from the machine into the crust. If your schedule doesn't allow this, however, you can certainly use already-made ice cream; you'll just need to soften it in the refrigerator and beat it in a stand mixer to get it to the optimal spreading consistency. (See page 26, step 2.)

## TOOLS

- 9-inch pie pan (glass, metal, or ceramic)
- A stand mixer with the paddle attachment, if using already-frozen ice cream
- A rubber spatula
- An offset metal spatula

## INGREDIENTS

- One baked and cooled Cookie Crumb Piecrust (at left)
- ¹/₃ cup inclusion such as nuts, chopped candies, sauce, or cookie pieces for the piecrust (optional; see page 27 for examples)
- About 1 quart (1 batch) ice cream
- Toppings to garnish the assembled pie (optional; see page 27 for examples)

## TIMELINE

- **Two days before:** Make a batch of ice cream base and chill. Pulverize the cookies of your choice (store-bought or homemade) in a food

Step 1

Step 2

Step 3

processor to make 1½ cups crumbs. Make and bake the piecrust (it can sit wrapped with plastic wrap overnight on the counter).

- **The day before:** Churn the ice cream and assemble the pie. Freeze overnight.
- **The morning of:** Decorate the pie with any desired frostings or garnishes and freeze until ready to serve.
- **5 minutes before:** Let the pie sit at room temperature before slicing.

## METHOD

1. **Spread the inclusions of your choice across the bottom of the crust (optional).** Sprinkle or drizzle it as evenly as possible.

2. **Add the ice cream.** If you have just-churned, soft ice cream, transfer it directly from the machine into the piecrust. If your ice cream has been stored in the freezer, allow it to soften in the refrigerator for 20 to 30 minutes; meanwhile, put the bowl of the stand mixer, the paddle attachment, and the piecrust in the freezer. Put the slightly softened ice cream in the mixing bowl and beat on low speed just until the ice cream is softened and malleable, about 30 seconds. (It doesn't need to be completely smooth, just spreadable.) Transfer the ice cream to the piecrust.

3. Use an offset spatula to nudge the ice cream all the way to the sides of the crust, filling any gaps or holes. Rap the filled pan gently (so as not to dislodge the cookie crumb crust) on the counter a few times to encourage any air bubbles to rise to the surface and smooth the top. Top the ice cream with any candies or nuts you want to add to the pie before freezing.

4. **Freeze the pie.** Put the assembled pie in the freezer and freeze overnight.

**TIP:** *For ice creams that contain swirled-in sauces (like the White Chocolate Raspberry Swirl on page 141), too much stirring or manipulation, including the process of building the ice cream pie, can produce muddy-looking results. If you want to use one of these flavors in an ice cream pie, just freeze the ice cream base as instructed by the recipe and incorporate the swirl once the ice cream is in the piecrust.*

5. **Decorate with the frosting, glaze, meringue, or whipped cream of your choice.** Work quickly so that the ice cream doesn't melt, and freeze until ready to serve.

6. **Serve the pie.** Remove the pie from the freezer 5 minutes before serving to soften it slightly. A hot, dry knife will yield the cleanest cuts. Dip your knife in a glass of hot water, wipe it clean with a towel, and cut a slice. Repeat between every slice.

## OUR FAVORITE ICE CREAM PIE COMBOS

*S'mores (shown below, at left)*
Piecrust made with Brown Sugar Graham Crackers (page 66)
Caramel Sauce (page 71)
Chocolate Ice Cream (page 78)
Meringue (page 50)

*Cookies and Cream (shown on page 97)*
Piecrust made with Dark Chocolate Cookies (page 90)
Cookies and Cream Ice Cream (page 84)
Chocolate Whipped Cream (page 96)
Chocolate Shavings (page 97)

*Blueberry Cheesecake (shown on page 40)*
Piecrust made with Brown Sugar Graham Crackers (page 66)
Cheesecake Ice Cream (page 41)
Fresh Blueberries, Berry Compote (page 148), or Blueberry-Lemon Sauce (page 150)

*Magic of the '80s (shown on page 140)*
Piecrust made with Shortbread (page 44)
White Chocolate Raspberry Swirl Ice Cream (page 141)
Extra Raspberry Swirl Sauce (page 142) for serving)

Step 5

### MAKE IT YOUR OWN

✤ Create your own ice cream pie by choosing your favorite piecrust, an ice cream flavor, and a topping.

# ICE CREAM SANDWICH ASSEMBLY

At Bi-Rite Creamery we use special silicone molds to create perfectly round "pucks" of ice cream for our ice cream sandwiches. However, you don't have to invest in these; the instructions below will help you make professional-looking ice cream sandwiches at home using regular kitchen equipment.

It's best to assemble ice cream sandwiches a few hours before you plan to serve them; the extra time in the freezer helps them freeze into a cohesive sandwich and helps prevent the ice cream from squishing out as you eat them.

## TOOLS

- A large rimmed baking sheet that fits in your freezer
- ½ cup dry measuring cup (optional)
- Small offset spatula (optional)

## INGREDIENTS

- Baked and cooled cookies of your choice (two cookies per sandwich)
- Ice cream (for 3-inch cookies, you'll need about ½ cup of ice cream per sandwich)

## TIME COMMITMENT

- 20 minutes to soften the ice cream
- At least 2 hours to solidify the assembled ice cream sandwiches

## METHOD

1. **Get the cookies ready.** Arrange half of the cookies upside down on a baking sheet.
2. **Prepare the ice cream and assemble.** Put the ice cream in the refrigerator for 20 minutes or so to let soften slightly (set the timer!).

   If you're the perfectionist type, you can get a more uniform shape by using a dry measuring cup as a mold for the ice cream. Pack the ice cream into a ½-cup dry measuring cup, then use a small spoon to nudge the "puck" of ice cream out onto the cookie. Use a small offset spatula to even out the top and smooth the sides. Top with the remaining cookies and press gently to adhere.

   Or, you can get a more handmade look by simply scooping a large scoop of ice cream onto a cookie and sandwiching it with the second cookie. Press on the cookies slightly to encourage the ice cream to come all the way to the edges.

3. **Freeze the sandwiches.** Put the baking sheet in the freezer and let the sandwiches harden for at least 2 hours.

   **TIP:** *For the crispest cookies and brightest flavors, assemble the sandwiches the same day you plan to eat them. You can assemble these up to 1 week ahead of time, but the cookies will soften and the flavors will mellow the longer the sandwiches are stored. If storing for longer than 1 day, transfer the hardened sandwiches to zip-top freezer bags or individual glassine bags, being sure to squeeze out any excess air before sealing.*

## OUR FAVORITE ICE CREAM SANDWICH COMBOS

Coconut Macaroons (page 208) with Chocolate Ice Cream (page 78)

Dark Chocolate Cookies (page 90) with Mint Chip Ice Cream (page 182)

Chocolate Chip Cookies (page 87) with Vanilla Ice Cream (page 35)

Lemon Gingersnaps (page 169) with Ginger Ice Cream (page 178) or Meyer Lemon Ice Cream (page 156)

Snickerdoodles (page 195) with Balsamic Strawberry Ice Cream (page 138)

Ice cream sandwiches with Meyer
Lemon Ice Cream (page 156) and
Lemon Gingersnaps (page 169)

# VANILLA

ONE OF THE CHALLENGES OF RUNNING a responsible business is finding ingredients that not only taste good but are also made in a way that is good for the earth and the people who produce the ingredients and work with them. Vanilla is particularly challenging in this respect. Like chocolate, it is a high-priced crop that changes hands many times before it reaches the consumer, making it difficult to get straight answers about how it was produced. During the course of writing this book, we began to source our vanilla from Madécasse, a Madagascar-based company committed not just to growing vanilla and chocolate that are of high quality but also to doing it in a sustainable manner. They pay farmers fair wages and centralize production in the same country where the ingredients are grown. We're so happy to support a company that not only sells products that taste amazing but is also redefining an entire industry for the better.

## TYPES OF VANILLA

Vanilla beans are the fruit of a climbing orchid vine native to Mexico but are now grown in tropical regions around the world. Each flower produces a single vanilla bean, and for commercial production, each flower must be pollinated by hand. As a result, vanilla is one of the most expensive spices in the world.

Vanilla is available in several different forms, and the recipe or technique you're using will dictate which form is most appropriate.

**Vanilla beans** are the most basic, unprocessed form of vanilla. Both the pod and the seeds inside are full of flavor, and the best way to coax it out is to split the bean lengthwise, scrape out the seeds and steep the seeds and bean in warm liquid. **Pure vanilla extract,** on the other hand, offers vanilla flavor in liquid form, which is useful for recipes where infusing vanilla beans into liquid is not an option.

These ingredients don't necessarily need to be used separately. In recipes where we want the maximum vanilla flavor possible (such as our vanilla ice cream), we use both vanilla beans and extract. This gives us the pronounced yet complex flavor profile that we want.

Aside from its physical form, you may have additional choices when buying vanilla. Just as *terroir* is considered an important factor that influences how a wine tastes, the place of origin is also considered a significant factor in the character of vanilla. (The specific variety of vanilla grown, the maturity of the beans at harvest, and the method of processing method also have some impact, but origin is the most influential variable on flavor.)

- Tahitian vanilla is fruity and has an almost licorice-like flavor. Note, however, that some producers use the word "Tahitian" to describe a type of vanilla plant even if it is grown outside Tahiti, so be sure to look carefully at the label to determine the true country of origin.

- Madagascar produces vanilla that is creamy and mellow in flavor.
- Mexican vanilla is slightly spicy and an especially good complement to chocolate.

If you can find vanilla beans or extract from several different origins, buy a few different ones and experiment with them to find your favorite. You may find that some are especially well suited to ice cream or sauces, while others really shine in cookies or cakes.

## BUYING AND USING VANILLA BEANS

More than likely, it will be most practical for you to buy whatever vanilla beans are available at your local grocery store (or specialty baking store, if you have one nearby). If that's the case, buy vanilla beans only as you need them; they have a tendency to dry out and become more difficult to use with age (unless you store them in neutral spirits, as described below).

If you see a lot of vanilla beans in your future, though, you may want to buy them in bulk through an online retailer. You'll have more options as to the origin and varietal of the beans (each of which has a unique flavor), the beans will be fresher, and you'll spend a lot less per bean. A few of these companies are listed in the Sources section (page 210).

If you do buy in bulk, store the beans submerged in a neutral spirit (such as vodka) in the refrigerator. This will not only extend their shelf life nearly indefinitely, but the beans will also infuse into the spirit, and you'll be producing your very own homemade vanilla extract.

Plump beans are much easier to work with and will yield the maximum flavor. If a vanilla bean has become dry and brittle, you can soften it by soaking it in a shallow bowl of warm water for 15 or 20 minutes.

Most recipes will instruct you to scrape the seeds from the pod before adding them both to the infusing liquid. This helps distribute the seeds evenly through the liquid and extracts the flavor more thoroughly.

After infusing, the pods are usually strained out and the tiny specklike seeds are left remaining in the liquid. Whatever you do, don't toss out those pods! They still have plenty of flavor left in them and can be reused in one of several different ways. Rinse them off and let them dry completely (you can speed the process by spreading them on a baking sheet and baking them at 250°F for 30 to 40 minutes). Then do one of the following:

- **Save the pods for later use in another recipe.** To store them, put the pods in a jar with enough vodka or other neutral spirit to cover and store at room temperature or in the refrigerator.

- **Make vanilla sugar or salt.** Combine the dried beans with sugar or salt in a food processor or blender and pulse until the beans are finely ground. Use anytime you'd like to add a subtle vanilla flavor to a recipe. The salt is wonderful sprinkled over freshly steamed fish, and the sugar is great in any dessert recipe!

## BUYING AND USING PURE VANILLA EXTRACT

The most important thing to know about vanilla extract is the difference between "vanilla flavoring" and pure vanilla extract. In a single vanilla bean there are more than two hundred different molecular compounds, all of which contribute to the incredibly complex flavor. Pure vanilla extract is made from actual vanilla beans, so the extract represents the full spectrum of vanilla flavor. On the other hand, "vanilla flavoring" consists of a sole flavor molecule, vanillin, which is derived from wood pulp. It tastes vanilla-ish, but it doesn't begin to represent the heady complexity of an actual vanilla bean. You will pay slightly more for pure vanilla extract, but it will make a significant difference in the final product. Be sure to watch out for blends that use a combination of real vanilla extract and vanillin—they are no substitute for the 100 percent real thing.

Most vanilla extract is alcohol-based, which gives it a nearly infinite shelf life. Just be sure to store it in a cool, dark place away from sunlight and heat.

Although it is easy to blend into batters and sauces, the flavor of vanilla extract has a tendency to dissipate and diminish, especially in the presence of heat. This is why we always add vanilla extract at the last possible stage of a recipe. For instance, when making our vanilla ice cream, we add the extract to the base just before it goes into the ice cream machine.

# VANILLA ICE CREAM

Makes about 1 quart

It always makes us happy when people get a scoop of our vanilla ice cream. Sure, it may not be quite as exciting as some of our other flavors, but to us vanilla is the true litmus test of a great ice cream maker. Vanilla gives you a pure sense of the quality of ingredients—not just of the vanilla itself, but also of the dairy products and eggs—as well as the skill of the ice cream maker.

We use two kinds of vanilla in this recipe, both vanilla bean and pure extract, for an intense vanilla flavor. This ice cream is the ideal canvas for any type of mix-ins you want to use, from chopped nuts, cookies, or candies to swirled-in sauces. Or keep it simple and enjoy the pure floral vanilla flavor!

## AT A GLANCE

| TECHNIQUE: | SPECIAL EQUIPMENT: | INFUSING AND CHILLING TIME: | SHELF LIFE: |
|---|---|---|---|
| Ice cream (page 12) | Ice cream machine | 30 minutes, plus 2 hours or overnight | 1 week |

1³/₄ cups heavy cream

³/₄ cup 1% or 2% milk

¹/₂ cup sugar

¹/₄ teaspoon kosher salt

1 vanilla bean

5 large egg yolks

2 teaspoons pure vanilla extract

### INFUSE THE MILK/CREAM

1. In a heavy nonreactive saucepan, stir together the cream, milk, half of the sugar (¹/₄ cup), and the salt. Split the vanilla bean lengthwise and use the knife to carefully scrape the seeds from the bean. Add the seeds and the split bean to the pan.

2. Put the pan over medium-high heat. When the mixture just begins to bubble around the edges, remove from the heat, cover the pan, and let steep for about 30 minutes.

### MAKE THE BASE

3. In a medium heatproof bowl, whisk the yolks just to break them up, then whisk in the remaining sugar (¹/₄ cup) until smooth. Set aside.

4. Uncover the cream mixture and put the pan over medium-high heat. When the mixture approaches a bare simmer, reduce the heat to medium.

5. Carefully scoop out about ¹/₂ cup of the hot cream mixture and, whisking the eggs constantly, add the cream to the bowl with the egg yolks. Repeat, adding another ¹/₂ cup of the hot cream to the bowl with the egg yolks. Using a heatproof rubber spatula, stir the cream in the saucepan as you slowly pour the egg-and-cream mixture from the bowl into the pan.

6. Cook the mixture carefully over medium heat, stirring constantly, until it is thickened, coats the back of a spatula or wooden spoon,

CONTINUED

Chocolate Chip
Vanilla Ice Cream

BERT CREAMERY

and holds a clear path when you run your finger across the spatula, 1 to 2 minutes longer.

7. Strain the base through a fine-mesh strainer into a clean container. Set the container into an ice-water bath, wash your spatula, and stir occasionally until the base is cool. Remove from the ice-water bath, cover with plastic wrap, and refrigerate the base for at least 2 hours or overnight.

### FREEZE THE ICE CREAM

8. Add the vanilla extract to the base and stir until blended.

9. Freeze in your ice cream machine according to the manufacturer's instructions. While the ice cream is churning, put the container you'll use to store the ice cream into the freezer. Enjoy right away or, for a firmer ice cream, transfer to the chilled container and freeze for at least 4 hours.

> **SERVE IT WITH . . .**
> ❋ A scoop of Tangerine Granita, as shown on page 166

# BUTTERMILK ICE CREAM

Makes about 1 quart

We think of this flavor as old-fashioned—in the best way possible. It evokes an earlier time, when butter was churned at home by hand. Buttermilk's tart-rich flavor enhances any kind of fruit.

## AT A GLANCE

| TECHNIQUE: | SPECIAL EQUIPMENT: | CHILLING TIME: | SHELF LIFE: |
|---|---|---|---|
| Ice cream (page 12) | Ice cream machine | 2 hours or overnight | 1 week |

5 large egg yolks

3/4 cup sugar

1 1/2 cups heavy cream

1/2 cup 1% or 2% milk

1 cup buttermilk

1 teaspoon pure vanilla extract

### MAKE THE BASE

1. In a medium heatproof bowl, whisk the yolks just to break them up, then whisk in half of the sugar (6 tablespoons). Set aside.

2. In a heavy nonreactive saucepan, stir together the cream, milk, and the remaining sugar (6 tablespoons) and put the pan over medium-high heat. When the mixture approaches a bare simmer, reduce the heat to medium.

3. Carefully scoop out about 1/2 cup of the hot cream mixture and, whisking the eggs constantly, add the cream to the bowl with the egg yolks. Repeat, adding another 1/2 cup of the hot cream to the bowl with the yolks. Using a heatproof rubber spatula, stir the cream in the saucepan as you slowly pour the egg-and-cream mixture from the bowl into the pan.

4. Cook the mixture carefully over medium heat, stirring constantly, until it is thickened, coats the back of a spatula, and holds a clear path when you run your finger across the spatula, 1 to 2 minutes longer.

5. Strain the base through a fine-mesh strainer into a clean container. Set the container into an ice-water bath, wash your spatula, and use it to stir the base occasionally until it is cool. Remove from the ice-water bath, cover with plastic wrap, and refrigerate the base for at least 2 hours or overnight.

   (The base must be completely cold, otherwise the buttermilk will cause the mixture to "break" and lose its emulsion.)

### FREEZE THE ICE CREAM

6. Add the buttermilk and vanilla to the cold base and whisk to blend.

7. Freeze in your ice cream machine according to the manufacturer's instructions. While the ice cream is churning, put the container you'll use to store the ice cream into the freezer. Enjoy right away or, for a firmer ice cream, transfer to the chilled container and freeze for at least 4 hours.

> **SERVE IT WITH . . .**
> ❋ A slice of fruit pie or galette or a simple fruit compote

# CRÈME FRAÎCHE ICE CREAM

Makes about 1 quart | Pictured on page 151

This luscious ice cream pairs well with many flavors, since the natural tanginess of crème fraîche offers a perfect neutral background for fruit. We make this in the late spring and early summer because it is such a perfect pairing for the strawberries, cherries, and other fruits that come in around that time. We have one guest, James, who stocks up on quarts of it when we approach the end of our run!

We prefer to make our own crème fraîche. It takes just a minute to mix the ingredients, then a day later they're cultured—and taste so good! This recipe makes a little more than you need to make the ice cream; use any leftovers slathered onto scones or even swirled into puréed soups. You could, of course, use store-bought crème fraîche if you don't have time to make it yourself.

## AT A GLANCE

| TECHNIQUE: | SPECIAL EQUIPMENT: | WAITING AND CHILLING TIME: | SHELF LIFE: |
|---|---|---|---|
| Ice cream (page 12) | Ice cream machine | 24 to 48 hours for the crème fraîche, 2 hours or overnight for the ice cream base | 1 week |

**FOR THE CRÈME FRAÎCHE**

1 cup heavy cream

3 tablespoons buttermilk

**FOR THE ICE CREAM**

4 large egg yolks

³/₄ cup sugar

1 cup heavy cream

1 cup 1% or 2% milk

¹/₄ teaspoon kosher salt

1 cup crème fraîche

2 tablespoons strained fresh lemon juice

### MAKE THE CRÈME FRAÎCHE

1. In a small bowl, mix the cream and buttermilk. Cover and let stand at room temperature for 24 to 48 hours, or until the consistency of sour cream. Then refrigerate until needed; the crème fraîche will become even thicker as it cools down.

**TIP:** *The warmer your kitchen, the faster the crème fraîche will thicken. If you aren't sure how long it will take, or if it's your first time making it, allot the full 48 hours just in case. If it takes less time than that to thicken, you can store it in the fridge for a few days until you're ready to use it.*

### MAKE THE BASE

2. In a medium heatproof bowl, whisk the yolks just to break them up, then whisk in half of the sugar (6 tablespoons). Set aside.

3. In a heavy nonreactive saucepan, combine the cream, milk, salt, and the remaining sugar (6 tablespoons) and put the pan over medium-high heat. When the mixture approaches a bare simmer, reduce the heat to medium.

4. Carefully scoop out about ¹/₂ cup of the hot cream mixture and, whisking the eggs

constantly, add the cream to the bowl with the egg yolks. Repeat, adding another ½ cup of the hot cream to the bowl with the yolks. Using a heatproof rubber spatula, stir the cream in the saucepan as you slowly pour the egg-and-cream mixture from the bowl into the pan.

5. Cook the mixture carefully over medium heat, stirring constantly, until it is thickened, coats the back of a spatula, and holds a clear path when you run your finger across the spatula, 1 to 2 minutes longer.

6. Strain the base through a fine-mesh strainer into a clean container. Set the container into an ice-water bath, wash your spatula, and use it to stir the base occasionally until it is cool. Remove from the ice-water bath, cover with plastic wrap, and refrigerate the base for at least 2 hours or overnight.

   (In this recipe, it's particularly important that the base is cold before proceeding to the next step, because otherwise the crème fraîche will cause the mixture to "break" and lose its emulsion.)

## FREEZE THE ICE CREAM

7. Add the crème fraîche and lemon juice to the cold base and whisk to blend.

8. Freeze in your ice cream machine according to the manufacturer's instructions. While the ice cream is churning, put the container you'll use to store the ice cream into the freezer. Enjoy right away or, for a firmer ice cream, transfer to the chilled container and freeze for at least 4 hours.

### SERVE IT WITH . . .
* Blood Orange Sorbet (page 162), one of Anne's favorite combinations
* Balsamic Strawberry Ice Cream (page 138) and Sliced Strawberry Topping (page 149)
* Chocolate Ice Cream (page 78)
* Lemon Gingersnaps (page 169)

Pie

blueberry

Yum.

Ice cream pie with Cheesecake Ice Cream, Brown Sugar
Graham Cracker piecrust (page 66), and fresh blueberries

# CHEESECAKE ICE CREAM

Makes about 1¹/₂ quarts

Whereas the buttermilk and crème fraîche ice creams are light and delicate, this one packs a rich, creamy wallop. This recipe is made for add-in ingredients to create a full-on cheesecake effect: see Make It Your Own (page 42) for ideas.

Plain cream cheese, like Philadelphia brand, is the classic choice for making this recipe; in fact, the stabilizers in this product will help keep the base emulsified. Natural cream cheese will give you a lighter flavor. Or use mascarpone for a rich flavor without the tang of cream cheese.

## AT A GLANCE

| TECHNIQUE: | SPECIAL EQUIPMENT: | CHILLING TIME: | SHELF LIFE: |
|---|---|---|---|
| Ice cream (page 12) | Ice cream machine | 2 hours or overnight | 1 week |

5 large egg yolks

³/₄ cup sugar

1¹/₂ cups heavy cream

1¹/₂ cups 1% or 2% milk

8 ounces cream cheese, at room temperature

1 tablespoon strained fresh lemon juice

1 teaspoon pure vanilla extract

### MAKE THE BASE

1. In a medium heatproof bowl, whisk the yolks just to break them up, then whisk in half of the sugar (6 tablespoons). Put the cream cheese in another medium heatproof bowl. Set both bowls aside.

2. In a heavy nonreactive saucepan, stir together the cream, milk, and the remaining sugar (6 tablespoons) and put the pan over medium-high heat. When the mixture approaches a bare simmer, reduce the heat to medium.

3. Carefully scoop out about ¹/₂ cup of the hot cream mixture and, whisking the eggs constantly, add the cream to the bowl with the egg yolks. Repeat, adding another ¹/₂ cup of the hot cream to the bowl with the yolks. Using a heatproof rubber spatula, stir the cream in the saucepan as you slowly pour the egg-and-cream mixture from the bowl into the pan.

4. Cook the mixture carefully over medium heat, stirring constantly, until it is thickened, coats the back of a spatula, and holds a clear path when you run your finger across the spatula, 1 to 2 minutes longer.

5. Strain the base through a fine-mesh strainer into the bowl with the cream cheese. Whisk until smooth, then set the bowl into an ice-water bath, wash your spatula, and use it to stir the base occasionally until it is cool. Remove from the ice-water bath, cover with plastic wrap, and refrigerate the base for at least 2 hours or overnight.

   (In this recipe, it's particularly important that the base is cold before proceeding to the next step, because otherwise the lemon juice will cause the mixture to "break" and lose its emulsion.)

CONTINUED

FREEZE THE ICE CREAM

6. Add the lemon juice and vanilla to the cold base and whisk to incorporate well.

7. Freeze in your ice cream machine according to the manufacturer's instructions. While the ice cream is churning, put the container you'll use to store the ice cream into the freezer. Enjoy right away or, for a firmer ice cream, transfer to the chilled container and freeze for at least 4 hours.

**MAKE IT YOUR OWN**
* Fold in 1/2 cup crumbled graham crackers.
* Swirl in 1/2 to 1/3 cup Raspberry Swirl Sauce (page 142), Fudge Ripple (page 122), or Lemon Curd (page 171).

**SERVE IT WITH . . .**
* Whatever toppings you like on your cheesecake, like Berry Compote (page 148) or Blueberry-Lemon Sauce (page 150)
* Our favorites, Hot Fudge Sauce (page 93) and Almond Toffee (page 68)

# GREAT YELLOW CAKE

Makes two 8-inch round cakes (enough for 2 ice cream cakes) or about 24 cupcakes

We use this as a base for many of our ice cream cakes, and it gets its name because it is so versatile. Our favorite combination? Soak the cake with some caramel sauce and top with a layer each of Brown Butter Pecan Ice Cream (page 124) and Malted Vanilla Ice Cream with Peanut Brittle and Milk Chocolate Pieces (page 126). Divine!

You can also skip the ice cream altogether and use this recipe to make a traditional layer cake for a birthday or any other celebration. Or bake the batter into cupcakes and top with buttercream frosting.

## AT A GLANCE

| | | |
|---|---|---|
| SPECIAL EQUIPMENT: Two round cake pans, each 8 inches in diameter and 2 inches deep, or two standard muffin pans | COOLING TIME: At least 1 hour | SHELF LIFE: 5 days |

Nonstick cooking spray or unsalted butter, for the pans

3/4 cup canola oil

1/2 cup water

1/3 cup apple juice

2 cups (9 ounces) unbleached all-purpose flour

1 tablespoon baking powder

1/2 teaspoon kosher salt

1 1/2 cups sugar

4 large eggs

1/4 teaspoon pure vanilla extract

1. Position a rack in the center of the oven if making cakes; if making cupcakes, position racks in the top and bottom thirds of the oven. Preheat the oven to 350°F. If making cakes, spray or butter two round cake pans, each 8 inches in diameter and 2 inches deep, and line the bottoms with parchment; if making cupcakes, line two standard muffin pans with paper or foil liners.

2. In a liquid measuring cup, mix the oil, water, and apple juice and set aside. In a medium bowl, whisk together the flour, baking powder, and salt and set that aside as well.

3. In the bowl of a stand mixer with the whisk attachment, combine the sugar, eggs, and vanilla. Whip on medium-high speed until the mixture is thick, has tripled in volume, and makes a fat ribbon that holds its shape for a few seconds on top of the batter when you lift the whisk, about 4 minutes.

4. With the motor running on medium speed, add the liquid in a slow, steady stream. (The trick here is to incorporate and emulsify the liquid into the eggs without causing the eggs to deflate. Adding the liquid slowly in a constant stream is the name of the game.)

5. Add the dry ingredients to the egg mixture and mix on low speed just until the batter is smooth and lump-free, about 30 seconds. (Be careful not to overbeat, which will make the cake tough.)

6. Divide the batter between the cake pans or among the muffin cups. Bake until the cakes are golden, spring back to a light touch, and a toothpick inserted into the center comes out clean, about 35 minutes for cake and about 20 minutes for cupcakes.

Great Yellow Cake as cupcakes

7. Let the cakes cool in the pans for 40 minutes, then invert onto a wire rack. Remove the parchment and let cool completely. Let the cupcakes cool in the pans for 20 minutes before transferring onto a wire rack, then let cool completely.

# SHORTBREAD

Makes about 28 two-inch cookies, or one 9- or 10-inch tart crust, or 4 cups of crumbs | Pictured as piecrust on page 140

This recipe is easy to follow, and mixing the dough takes no time at all. You can use it to make buttery, crumbly cookies to serve with ice cream or a tart crust, which is especially good filled with lemon curd, whipped cream, or pastry cream, and topped with fresh fruit. This shortbread can also be used to make a Cookie Crumb Piecrust (page 25) for an ice cream pie.

## AT A GLANCE

CHILLING TIME: 2 hours or up to overnight if making cookies or tart crust

SHELF LIFE: 5 days for cookies and crust, 1 week for crumbs

1 cup (8 ounces) cold unsalted butter, cut into ¹/₂-inch cubes

2 cups (9 ounces) unbleached all-purpose flour, plus more for dusting

¹/₂ cup powdered sugar, measured then sifted

¹/₂ teaspoon kosher salt

### MAKE THE DOUGH

1. Combine all of the ingredients in the bowl of a stand mixer with the paddle attachment. Mix on low speed at first, and then increase to medium-low speed and continue mixing until the dough is smooth and just comes together in a solid mass, 1¹/₂ to 2 minutes.

### TO MAKE COOKIES

2. Turn the dough out onto a piece of plastic wrap and shape into a disk 1 inch thick. Wrap in the plastic wrap and refrigerate until firm, 1 to 2 hours or up to overnight.

3. When you're ready to bake, position racks in the top and bottom thirds of the oven and preheat the oven to 350°F. Line two baking sheets with parchment paper or nonstick mats.

4. On a lightly floured surface, roll the dough to a ¹/₄-inch thickness (or slightly thicker or thinner, if you like). Using a cookie cutter (or a knife for free-form shapes), cut out cookies from the dough. If you use a cutter, gather and reroll the scraps up to two more times; any more than that and the cookies will become tough.

5. Arrange the cookies at least ³/₄ inch apart on the baking sheets and bake for 8 minutes. Rotate the sheets top to bottom and front to back and continue to bake until lightly browned around the edges, 4 to 6 minutes longer.

6. Let cool on the baking sheets for 5 minutes, then gently transfer to a rack (the cookies are very delicate when warm, but will become slightly sturdier as they cool). Let cool completely.

   Store in an airtight container.

### TO MAKE A TART CRUST

2. Turn the dough out onto a piece of plastic wrap and shape into a disk 1 inch thick. Wrap in the plastic wrap and refrigerate until firm, 1 to 2 hours or up to overnight.

3. When you're ready to bake, position a rack in the center of the oven and preheat the oven to 350°F.

4. On a lightly floured surface, roll the dough to a ¼-inch thickness. Transfer to a tart pan 9 or 10 inches in diameter either by rolling the dough loosely around the rolling pin and unrolling over the pan, or by sliding the removable tart pan bottom under the dough and using it to transfer the dough into the pan. Being careful not to press or stretch the dough, gently ease the dough into the corners of the pan. Remove the excess dough along the top edge of the pan using a small knife or your fingers. Prick the bottom of the dough with a fork at 1-inch intervals.

5. Bake until the crust is light golden and looks dry in the center, about 20 minutes. When you take it out of the oven, gently press down on any air bubbles that may have formed. Let cool completely on a rack.

## TO MAKE CRUMBS FOR AN ICE CREAM PIE

2. Position racks in the top and bottom thirds of the oven and preheat the oven to 350°F. Line two baking sheets with parchment paper or nonstick mats.

3. Break the dough into walnut-sized lumps with your fingers and space them evenly on the baking sheets. Bake for 10 minutes, then rotate the pans front to back and top to bottom. Continue to bake for another 10 to 15 minutes, or until the pieces are golden brown and give just slightly to the touch.

4. Let cool completely on the baking sheets. Working in batches as necessary, transfer the shortbread to a food processor and pulse until it becomes a coarse meal. Store in an airtight container for up to a week at room temperature; freeze for longer storage.

# SUGAR CONES *or* BOWLS

Makes about 15 cones or bowls

These crispy, delicious cones taste better than anything you can buy. Best of all, you don't need a special machine to make your own sugar cones. All you need is a mold to shape the cones on, which you can easily make on your own (instructions follow this recipe), and a nonstick mat.

A small offset spatula is essential for spreading the batter as thinly as possible (the cones won't be crunchy if the batter is too thick). These cones are best eaten the same day they are made.

## AT A GLANCE

SPECIAL EQUIPMENT: Nonstick baking mat, a small offset spatula, and the mold of your choice (a metal or wooden cone shaper, a homemade shaper, or a teacup)

SHELF LIFE: 1 day

1¼ cups (6 ounces) powdered sugar, measured then sifted

½ cup egg whites (from about 4 large eggs)

¾ cup plus 2 tablespoons (4 ounces) unbleached all-purpose flour

½ cup (4 ounces) unsalted butter, melted

**MAKE IT YOUR OWN**

❊ Whisk 2 tablespoons finely grated lemon or orange zest into the flour before you stir it into the batter.

1. Position a rack in the center of the oven and preheat the oven to 350°F. Line a baking sheet with a nonstick mat.

2. Combine the powdered sugar and egg whites in a medium mixing bowl and whisk together. Add the flour, mix to blend, and add the melted butter. Mix again until blended and smooth.

3. Put a scant 2 tablespoons of batter in one corner of the nonstick mat and use a small offset spatula to spread the batter to a thin circle 5 inches in diameter. Try to spread the batter thinly and evenly for maximum crispiness.

   Repeat up to three more times, as the baking sheet allows. You can place them fairly close together, since they don't spread when baking, but you shouldn't bake more than four at a time, because otherwise the baked circles will harden before you're able to shape them all.

4. Bake for 6 to 7 minutes, rotating the pan during the last few minutes to help the cones brown evenly, until the edges of the batter are golden brown. Meanwhile, wash and dry the spatula.

### TO MAKE CONES

**5.** As soon as the baking sheet comes out of the oven, use the offset spatula to lift one of the circles and place it upside down on a work surface. Center the cone mold on the circle with the point about ¼ inch in from one edge. Quickly lift one side of the cookie, wrap it around the form, and repeat with the other side. (Use light fingers because the circle will be hot!) Gently pinch the point to close the end. Let the cone sit on the mold for a few seconds, then gently slide it off and repeat with the remaining circles. If one of the circles starts to firm up before you can form it, put the pan back in the oven for 30 seconds to reheat and soften it.

### TO MAKE BOWLS

**5.** Set a teacup upside down on the counter. As soon as the cookie sheet comes out of the oven, place a warm cookie over the cup. Use your hands to gently press the cookie down toward the sides of the teacup. Let cool for a second and repeat with the remaining circles.

## MAKING AN ICE CREAM CONE MOLD

Trace this pattern and transfer it to a piece of thin cardboard (the thickness of a cereal box is ideal). Roll the cardboard into a cone and use packing tape to secure the seam. Fill the cone with dried beans or uncooked rice and seal the top with tape. Then wrap in aluminum foil. You're now ready to make cones!

# VANILLA BUTTERSCOTCH SAUCE

Makes about 1½ cups

Butterscotch is a variation on a caramel sauce; it starts with a fairly light caramel for a delicate toasty base, and then it's enriched with the addition of butter. This sauce is irresistible drizzled over a couple of scoops of ice cream, or nibbled right off the spoon. Serve it warm, when it's thick and pourable; it takes on a pleasant, slightly chewy consistency when it comes in contact with cold ice cream.

## AT A GLANCE

TECHNIQUE: Variation on caramel (page 56)  SHELF LIFE: 2 weeks (or longer!)

½ cup heavy cream, at room temperature
½ vanilla bean
½ cup water
¼ teaspoon cream of tartar
1½ cups sugar
¼ cup (2 ounces) unsalted butter, cut into ½-inch slices
Pinch of kosher salt

1. Set the cream by the stove so it's at hand when you need it.

2. Split the vanilla bean lengthwise and use the knife to carefully scrape the seeds from the pod. Put the seeds and the split pod in a medium nonreactive saucepan.

   Add the water and cream of tartar to the pan and carefully pour the sugar into the center of the bottom of the pan. Do not stir.

3. Put the pan over medium-high heat. At this point you must watch the sugar constantly because once the caramelization begins the mixture can burn in a matter of moments! Cook without stirring until the sugar begins to brown in spots, 8 to 11 minutes. Gently swirl the pan once to evenly distribute the contents.

4. When the caramel is a light amber color (just a little darker than honey), about 5 minutes longer, remove the pan from the heat and immediately but slowly pour the cream into the pan. (The mixture will steam and bubble up, so wear oven mitts and be very careful to avoid splatters and steam burns.)

   When the bubbling subsides, gently stir to completely blend the cream into the caramel, scraping the vanilla bean seeds from the sides of the pan back into the sauce. If you have lumps of hardened caramel in your pan, put the pan over low heat and stir until the caramel is melted.

5. With a fork, carefully remove the vanilla pod from the sauce (it will be very hot!). Add the butter and salt and stir gently to blend. Let cool until just warm. If not using within a few hours, transfer to a container and refrigerate. Rewarm before using.

> **MAKE IT YOUR OWN**
> ❋ Make it boozy! Add a couple of tablespoons of scotch or bourbon along with the butter and salt. (We've dubbed this spiked version "Boozerscotch"!)

# VANILLA BUTTERCREAM FROSTING

Makes 4 cups (enough to frost a two-layer 8-inch cake, 24 cupcakes, or 2 or 3 ice cream cakes)

There are many different types of buttercream out there, but we like this one best. It's an old-fashioned version, made simply by combining the ingredients in a mixer and whipping until light and fluffy. It's not as fussy as other buttercream recipes and is more stable. This recipe can easily be halved.

AT A GLANCE

SHELF LIFE: Up to 2 weeks

1/2 vanilla bean

4 1/2 cups (1 1/2 pounds) powdered sugar, measured then sifted

2 cups (1 pound) unsalted butter, at warm room temperature and cut into 1/2-inch slices

1 tablespoon pure vanilla extract

1/2 teaspoon kosher salt

> **MAKE IT YOUR OWN**
> * For cinnamon buttercream, add 1 tablespoon ground cinnamon.
> * Fold in finely chopped peanut brittle, toffee, or chocolate.

1. Split the vanilla bean lengthwise and use the same knife to carefully scrape the seeds from the pod. Add the vanilla seeds and pod to the bowl of a stand mixer. Add the remaining ingredients to the mixing bowl and fit the mixer with the paddle attachment.

2. Beat first on low speed, and then increase to medium-high speed and continue to beat until the frosting is light, fluffy, and smooth, 2 to 3 minutes. Scrape the sides of the bowl and mix briefly again.

3. Remove the vanilla bean. Use the frosting immediately or cover and refrigerate for up to 2 weeks. If made ahead, let the frosting come to room temperature before using and remix briefly using the stand mixer until it regains its light and fluffy consistency.

# MERINGUE

Makes about 3 1/2 cups (enough to cover two 8-inch cakes) | Pictured on page 26

This quick-to-make meringue is a lovely finish to ice cream cakes and pies, plus it holds up in the freezer beautifully after you've assembled the dessert. Whenever we have leftover meringue, we use it to make a s'more sundae. We combine chocolate ice cream with our housemade graham crackers and caramel sauce, then we top it with meringue and toast it with our propane torch. You can also use this meringue to top lemon curd tarts or pies.

If you don't have a kitchen torch, you can toast the meringue in your oven under the broiler. You must keep a close eye on it though, because it burns easily and the ice cream will quickly start to melt!

## AT A GLANCE

SPECIAL EQUIPMENT: Propane or butane kitchen torch (not essential but very helpful)

SHELF LIFE: None; use immediately!

---

1/2 cup egg whites (from about 4 large eggs)

1 cup sugar

1/8 teaspoon kosher salt

> **TIP:** *Any type of oil or fat can hinder your whites from whipping up, so make sure your egg whites have no traces of yolk in them, and make sure your mixing bowl and whisk are spotlessly clean as well.*

### WARM THE EGG WHITES AND SUGAR

1. Put about 2 inches of water in the bottom of a medium saucepan and bring to a simmer over medium-high heat. If you are using a gas stove, make sure the flames are not coming up around the pan, which will cause the egg whites to scorch.

2. In the bowl of a stand mixer, whisk together the egg whites, sugar, and salt just until combined. Place the bowl over but not touching the simmering water. Whisk the whites occasionally until they are just warm to the touch and the sugar is completely dissolved (you should not be able to feel granules), about 3 minutes.

### WHIP THE MERINGUE

3. Place the bowl on the mixer fitted with the whisk attachment and whisk on medium speed until the whites are glossy and hold their shape, 4 to 5 minutes. (To test if they are ready, with the mixer off, dip your finger in the meringue and then remove it. When you pull up, the meringue should hold its shape in a soft peak that curves downward at the top.)

### DECORATE

4. Working quickly, spread the meringue over the top of the cake or pie you are decorating. Use the back of a spatula to create swirls and swoops in the meringue.

   Toast the meringue with a torch or under the broiler for a few seconds, just until the surface is lightly toasted.

# WHIPPED CREAM

Makes about 2 cups (enough for 6 to 8 sundaes)

Homemade whipped cream is vastly preferable to anything you buy at the store. The homemade kind actually tastes like cream, and you have control over how sweet it will be.

Once you whip the cream, it will hold for up to 8 hours in the refrigerator. It will separate as it sits, so rewhip the cream briefly just before using.

## AT A GLANCE
SHELF LIFE: 1 day

1 cup heavy cream
2 tablespoons sugar
1 teaspoon pure vanilla extract

Combine all of the ingredients in the bowl of a stand mixer and refrigerate for at least 15 minutes. (Doing this helps the cream whip faster.) Fit the bowl onto the mixer with the whisk attachment and whisk on medium-high speed until the cream is light and fluffy and holds a medium to firm peak when you lift the whisk out of the bowl, 2 to 3 minutes.

**TIP:** *Be careful not to overwhip the cream or its fat will start to coagulate into butter! It helps to reduce the mixer speed to medium as the cream approaches the desired consistency, thus slowing down the process and giving you a bigger window in which to pull the plug.*

**TIP:** *You can use half a vanilla bean instead of the vanilla extract. Split the bean lengthwise, scrape the seeds from the pod, and add the pod and seeds to the mixing bowl along with the cream and sugar. Remove the vanilla pod before using the whipped cream.*

# MARSHMALLOWS

Makes about 4 dozen 1¹/₂-inch marshmallows

This recipe requires a bit of time and attention, but it's all worth it to have homemade marshmallows. Our version uses simple, straightforward ingredients, including real vanilla and egg whites (most commercial marshmallows no longer contain them). This is the perfect place to showcase the nuanced flavors of a vanilla bean.

Timing is of the essence in this recipe, so it's critical to have all of the ingredients and equipment set out and ready at the start. A candy thermometer is also essential.

Use these marshmallows to make rocky road ice cream, float them on your hot chocolate, or mix them into fudge.

## AT A GLANCE

**SPECIAL EQUIPMENT:** Candy thermometer and offset spatula

**COOLING TIME:** Overnight, plus an additional hour as needed

**SHELF LIFE:** 2 weeks

---

Nonstick cooking spray, for the pan

About ¹/₂ cup powdered sugar, measured then sifted, for dusting

About ¹/₂ cup cornstarch, measured then sifted, for dusting

¹/₂ cup egg whites (from about 4 large eggs)

2 envelopes (¹/₄ ounce each) unflavored powdered gelatin

6 tablespoons water, plus more as needed

1¹/₄ cups granulated sugar

2 teaspoons pure vanilla extract or seeds from ¹/₂ vanilla bean

### GET READY

1. Spray a 9 by 13-inch baking pan with nonstick cooking spray and line it with parchment paper so that you have 1 inch of overhang on each long side of the pan. (The spray will help keep the parchment in place.) In a small bowl, mix the powdered sugar and cornstarch. Sift about 4 tablespoons of the powdered sugar–cornstarch mixture over the bottom of the pan and set aside.

2. Put the egg whites in the bowl of a stand mixer with the whisk attachment; you'll come back to it in a few minutes.

3. Put the gelatin in a shallow bowl and sprinkle 3 tablespoons of the water over it. Make sure the gelatin is completely saturated, adding a bit more water if necessary and using your fingers to gently mix it if needed. It will quickly thicken and become gummy and translucent.

### MAKE THE SYRUP AND WHIP THE WHITES

4. In a small heavy saucepan, mix the granulated sugar with the remaining 3 tablespoons water; the texture should be similar to wet sand. Use water-dipped fingers or a wet pastry brush to wash down the sides of the pan (this will help prevent the sugar from crystallizing) and attach a candy thermometer to the pan.

5. Put the pan over medium heat and cook, without stirring, until the mixture reaches 210°F, about 4 minutes. At this point let the syrup continue to cook over medium heat while you turn to the egg whites.

6. Whisk the egg whites on medium-high speed until they just form soft peaks, about 1½ minutes. When you lift the whisk out of the whites, they should hold their shape in a peak that droops over at the top.

**TIP:** *Egg whites can overwhip quickly, going from perfect peaks to grainy and unpleasant in an instant. If you're new to whipping whites, go on medium speed to slow down the process, making it easier to know when to say when.*

7. Once the whites reach soft peaks, reduce the speed to low and let them continue to mix as you return your attention to the syrup on the stove.

8. When the syrup reaches 238°F, also known as the "soft ball" stage, about 6 minutes total, remove the pan from the heat. Stir in the gelatin and the vanilla extract or seeds, making sure the gelatin is completely dissolved.

9. Increase the mixer speed to medium-high and slowly add the syrup to the whipping whites; the best way to avoid spattering is to pour it slowly down one side of the bowl. If some of the syrup does splatter or stick to the sides, just leave it; don't try to scrape it down.

   Continue to whip until the mixture has cooled somewhat (the bowl will still feel warm), 5 to 7 minutes longer.

SPREADING THE MARSHMALLOWS

10. Transfer the still-warm mixture to the prepared pan and spread evenly using an offset spatula. Sift about 4 tablespoons more powdered sugar–cornstarch mixture over the entire surface of the marshmallows. Let dry uncovered at room temperature overnight.

**TIP:** *Try to avoid dislodging the powdered sugar-cornstarch mixture on the bottom of the pan as you spread it around.*

11. The next day, invert the marshmallows onto a cutting board (gently pull on the overhanging parchment if the marshmallows don't immediately release from the pan). Peel off the parchment. Sift another 4 tablespoons powdered sugar–cornstarch mixture over the surface that was previously in contact with the parchment; if it seems tacky, let air dry for another hour or so before proceeding.

12. Using kitchen shears or a knife, cut the marshmallows into pieces of whatever size you desire. If the knife or scissors become sticky, dip in the powdered sugar–cornstarch mixture between slices or spray with non-stick cooking spray, which makes the job much easier.

13. Roll the marshmallows in more powdered sugar–cornstarch mixture, if you like. Store between layers of parchment in an airtight container.

**MAKE IT YOUR OWN**
* Use ¼ teaspoon peppermint extract in place of the vanilla extract or seeds. This variation is especially good in hot chocolate!

# CARAMEL

**WE HAVE AN INSIDE JOKE AT BI-RITE CREAMERY,** which is that we should have just named the shop "Caramel." After all, it's rare that anyone mentions our shop without also uttering the name of our best-selling ice cream flavor: Salted Caramel.

Before we opened our doors, we kept hearing the same advice from other shop owners: make three times as much vanilla ice cream as you think you will need. But, much to our surprise, it was the Salted Caramel that guests could never get enough of. It developed a cultlike following overnight, and we found ourselves making it more and more frequently just to keep up with the demand.

We figured out pretty quickly that this flavor should always be in our lineup, but in those early days we did run out a couple of times. And on those few occasions, there were people who would walk in, see that empty bin of Salted Caramel, and walk right out of the store. They didn't even want to try another flavor!

Caramel is essentially melted and toasted sugar, and it's that toasting that gives caramel its color and delicious, complex flavor. The darker the caramel, the more intense the flavor, which is why we take our caramel to a very dark stage. The flavor is more intriguing and unique that way, and it also ensures that the flavor doesn't get lost once we mix it into the ice cream base or other ingredients.

There are two ways of making caramel: the wet method (which uses water) and the dry (which uses sugar only). We prefer the dry method because we're able to take the caramel

to a much darker stage, giving us that more intense flavor. The dry method is also *much* faster, which is important considering how much of it we make. We use up to thirty pounds of sugar every day just for caramel, so those saved minutes add up!

You have to be really careful when making caramel. For one thing, the sugar gets crazy hot and can cause serious burns. Timing is also of the essence. A delay of just a few seconds can turn a lovely mahogany caramel into a black burned mess, and when that happens there's no saving it. You have to start over. That's not to say that making caramel is difficult. It just means you have to get your ducks in a row before you begin.

## BASIC CARAMEL TECHNIQUE

Most of the recipes in this chapter make use of the same basic recipe for caramel. (The only exception is the toffee recipe; it uses a different process but results in the same caramel flavor.) Here are some tips to keep in mind when making caramel.

- **Put everything in place before you turn on the stove.** Measure all of the ingredients and put all the necessary equipment within easy reach.

- **Once you turn on that burner, don't walk away.** Don't answer the phone, and resist flipping through the rest of this book!

- **Take action the very instant your caramel reaches the desired color.** Because caramel gets so hot, it continues to cook and darken rapidly even after you take the pan off the heat. To capture just the right hue of caramel (and to prevent burning), we stop the cooking by adding cream to the mixture. So when your caramel gets to the right color, don't delay and add the cream right away.

## TOOLS AND INGREDIENTS

You'll need the following to make caramel.

- **A deep, heavy, flat-bottomed, not-nonstick saucepan.** The extra depth helps prevent the caramel from overflowing, and a heavy gauge and flat bottom will ensure even cooking. Cookware that is *not* nonstick is better suited to high temperatures. Light-colored (silvery) pans make it easier to judge how dark your caramel is getting. Our recipes were tested using a 4-quart stainless steel–lined saucepan.

- **A wooden spoon.** Wood is ideal because it doesn't conduct heat and will not melt.

- **Oven mitts.** Not only are they necessary for handling the hot saucepan, but they also help protect your hands from spatters.

- **A bowl of ice water.** If you get hot sugar on your skin, dunking it in ice water is the best way to halt and soothe a burn.

- **Sugar.** We use organic granulated sugar at the Creamery, but we find that organic sugar is a bit fussier and burns more easily when making caramel. Conventional granulated sugar is a more foolproof option for these recipes.

# THE ULTIMATE TRIBUTE

The ultimate tribute to our ice cream came on Halloween a few years ago. A couple of neighborhood fans came into the shop to show us their costumes: they dressed as pint containers of our ice cream, one flavored as Salted Caramel and the other as Honey Lavender! It was obvious they had put a lot of work into faithfully re-creating our packaging, and for us it was quite an honor.

- **Heavy cream.** Adding the cream will cause the caramel to bubble and sputter furiously, but we've found that using room temperature cream causes less bubbling than cold cream, so be sure to set out your cream well before you start cooking the sugar.

## THE METHOD

1. Put 2 tablespoons of sugar in your saucepan and put the pan over medium-high heat. Let it sit undisturbed until the sugar starts to melt on the edges and you get a few darkish bubbles in the center.

2. Give the sugar a gentle stir—just enough to help the sugar melt and brown evenly. Let the sugar continue to caramelize, stirring occasionally. If the sugar seems to be cara-melizing too fast or threatening to burn, you can reduce the heat at any time in the process.

3. When the sugar is mostly melted and a nice dark amber color, stir in another 2 table-spoons sugar. Working in 2-tablespoon increments, continue to add the sugar, stir-ring frequently and allowing each batch of sugar to melt and caramelize before adding the next. (Once you get that initial batch of sugar melted and caramelized, subsequent additions of sugar will go pretty quickly.)

4. Once all the sugar is added, let the caramel continue to cook, stirring just enough to help it darken evenly. During this stage it may look lumpy, and it will eventually become frothy on the surface and start smoking, so don't be alarmed.

5. The very instant the caramel turns very dark mahogany—almost reddish in color—pull the pan off the heat and slowly and carefully add the cream. The mixture will bubble and sputter vigorously, so maintain an arm's distance as you add it. (If the caramel "seizes up" and solidifies at this point, just heat it gently over low heat until the sugar dissolves into the cream. This process could take up to 10 minutes.)

6. When the bubbling subsides, stir gently until the caramel and cream are completely blended and smooth. Again, if there are any stubborn lumps that won't dissolve, put the pan over low heat until they do. The caramel will stay rippin' hot for quite a while, so let it cool completely before giving it a taste.

Step 5

Step 5, continued

Step 6

# SALTED CARAMEL ICE CREAM

Makes about 1 quart

This flavor was a hit from the day we opened our doors, and it continues to be one of our most popular flavors. Every week we make about 135 pounds of caramel just for this ice cream.

Although salt and caramel might sound like a strange combination, it actually works marvelously: the slight bitterness of the dark caramel pulls your tastebuds in one direction while the salt pushes them in another, and the sweet cream rounds everything out. It's a wallop of flavor, and incredibly addictive.

## AT A GLANCE

| TECHNIQUES: | SPECIAL EQUIPMENT: | CHILLING TIME: | SHELF LIFE: |
|---|---|---|---|
| Ice cream (page 12), Caramel (page 56) | Ice cream machine | 2 hours, or overnight | 1 week |

1³/₄ cups heavy cream, at room temperature

³/₄ cup granulated sugar

³/₄ cup 1% or 2% milk

1 teaspoon kosher salt

5 large egg yolks

### MAKE THE CARAMEL

1. Set the cream by the stove so it's at hand when you need it. Measure out ¹/₂ cup of the sugar and set near the stove; you'll use this for the caramel (the rest will go in with the yolks). Put 2 tablespoons of the sugar for the caramel in a heavy nonreactive saucepan and put the pan over medium-high heat. When the sugar is melted around the edges and starts to turn amber in places (about 2 minutes), stir the mixture gently and add another 2 tablespoons sugar to the pan.

2. Continue to add what remains of the ¹/₂ cup of sugar 2 tablespoons at a time, stirring frequently and allowing most of the sugar to melt before you add more. Watch carefully as the sugar darkens, stirring gently to help it melt evenly.

3. When the caramel becomes a dark mahogany color, remove the pan from the heat and immediately but slowly pour the cream into the pan. (The mixture will steam and bubble up, so wear oven mitts and be very careful to avoid splatters and steam burns.) When the bubbling subsides, gently stir to completely blend the cream into the caramel. If you have lumps of hardened caramel in your pan, simply put the pan over low heat and stir until the caramel is melted.

### MAKE THE BASE

4. Once the caramel is completely smooth, stir in the milk along with the salt and put the pan over medium-high heat. When the mixture approaches a bare simmer, reduce the heat to medium.

5. In a medium heatproof bowl, whisk the yolks just to break them up, then whisk in the remaining ¹/₄ cup sugar. Set aside.

CONTINUED

6. Carefully scoop out about ½ cup of the hot cream mixture and, whisking the eggs constantly, add the cream to the bowl with the egg yolks. Repeat, adding another ½ cup of the hot cream to the bowl with the yolks. Using a heatproof rubber spatula, stir the cream in the saucepan as you slowly pour the egg-and-cream mixture from the bowl into the pan.

7. Cook the mixture carefully over medium heat, stirring constantly, until it is thickened, coats the back of a spatula, and holds a clear path when you run your finger across the spatula, 1 to 2 minutes longer.

8. Strain the base through a fine-mesh strainer into a clean container. Set the container into an ice-water bath, wash your spatula, and use it to stir the base occasionally until it is cool. Remove the container from the ice-water bath, cover with plastic wrap, and refrigerate the base for at least 2 hours or overnight.

### FREEZE THE ICE CREAM

9. When the base is completely chilled, freeze in your ice cream machine according to the manufacturer's instructions. While the ice cream is churning, put the container you'll use to store the ice cream into the freezer. Enjoy right away or, for a firmer ice cream, transfer to the chilled container and freeze for at least 4 hours.

**NOTE:** This ice cream has a much softer consistency than other ice creams due to its higher sugar content, and as a result it does not work well in ice cream cakes and pies. Save this one for scooping.

**SERVE IT WITH . . .**
- Crème Fraîche Ice Cream (page 38)
- Coffee Toffee Ice Cream (variation of recipe on page 103)
- Honey Lavender Ice Cream (page 180)— a favorite combination of our guests!
- Hot Fudge Sauce (page 93) and Marcona almonds

# BROWN SUGAR ICE CREAM *with* A GINGER-CARAMEL SWIRL

Makes about 1 quart | Pictured on page 65

Kris loves to tinker with ice cream. Every time she tries a new flavor that she loves, she goes home and re-creates it with her own spin, like with this recipe. The original was good in theory, but it was overloaded with candied ginger and gingerbread and simply had too much going on. Kris thought, "If it just focused on a few ingredients, it would be so much better." The result is proof that the simple combination of brown sugar, ginger, and caramel is all you need for an amazing explosion of flavor.

This started out as a Christmas flavor because it pairs so nicely with spiced things like gingerbread. After the holidays were over and we stopped making it, people demanded that we bring it back, so now it's always in the case and our guests enjoy it all year long.

## AT A GLANCE

| TECHNIQUES: | SPECIAL EQUIPMENT: | CHILLING TIME: | SHELF LIFE: |
|---|---|---|---|
| Ice cream (page 12), Caramel (page 56) | Ice cream machine | 2 hours or overnight | 1 week |

5 large egg yolks

1/2 cup packed dark brown sugar

1 3/4 cup heavy cream

3/4 cup 1% or 2% milk

1/4 teaspoon kosher salt

**FOR THE SWIRL**

3/4 cup heavy cream

1 cup granulated sugar

1 teaspoon jarred ginger spread (see Note, page 64)

1/8 teaspoon kosher salt

### MAKE THE BASE

1. In a medium heatproof bowl, whisk the yolks just to break them up, then whisk in half of the brown sugar (1/4 cup). Set aside.

2. In a heavy nonreactive saucepan, stir together the cream, milk, salt, and the remaining brown sugar (1/4 cup) and put the pan over medium-high heat. When the mixture approaches a bare simmer, reduce the heat to medium.

3. Carefully scoop out about 1/2 cup of the hot cream mixture and, whisking the eggs constantly, add the cream to the bowl with the egg yolks. Repeat, adding another 1/2 cup of the hot cream to the bowl with the yolks. Using a heatproof rubber spatula, stir the cream in the saucepan as you slowly pour the egg-and-cream mixture from the bowl into the pan.

4. Cook the mixture carefully over medium heat, stirring constantly, until it is thickened, coats the back of a spatula, and holds a clear path when you run your finger across the spatula, 1 to 2 minutes longer.

5. Strain the base through a fine-mesh strainer into a clean container. Set the container into an ice-water bath, wash your spatula, and use it to stir the base occasionally until

CONTINUED

it is cool. Remove the container from the ice-water bath, cover with plastic wrap, and refrigerate the base for at least 2 hours or overnight.

### WHILE THE ICE CREAM BASE COOLS, MAKE THE SWIRL

6. Set the cream by the stove so it's at hand when you need it. Put 2 tablespoons of the sugar in a heavy nonreactive saucepan, and put the pan over medium-high heat. When the sugar is melted around the edges and starts turn amber in places (about 2 minutes), stir the mixture gently and add another 2 tablespoons sugar to the pan.

7. Continue to add the remaining sugar 2 tablespoons at a time, stirring frequently and allowing most of the sugar to melt before you add more. Watch carefully as the sugar darkens, stirring gently to help it melt evenly.

   **TIP:** *Keep in mind that the flavor of the ice cream hinges on how dark you take the caramel. We take ours to a very dark, almost reddish, stage, which produces our intense signature flavor.*

8. When the caramel becomes a dark mahogany color, remove the pan from the heat and immediately but slowly pour the cream into the pan. (The mixture will steam and bubble up, so wear oven mitts and be very careful to avoid splatters and steam burns.) When the bubbling subsides, gently stir to completely blend the cream into the caramel. If you have lumps of hardened caramel in your pan, simply put the pan over low heat and stir until the caramel is melted.

9. Stir in the ginger paste and salt and let cool. (You can make the swirl up to 2 weeks ahead of time. Keep it refrigerated, but let it come to room temperature before using.)

### FREEZE THE ICE CREAM

10. When the base is completely chilled, freeze in your ice cream machine according to the manufacturer's instructions. While the ice cream is churning, put the container you'll use to store the ice cream into the freezer.

11. As you transfer the ice cream to the storage container, drizzle in the caramel after every few scoopfuls, using about 6 tablespoons of the caramel (or more if you like). When all the ice cream is in the container, use a chopstick or butter knife to gently swirl the mixture. Enjoy right away or, for a firmer ice cream, freeze for at least 4 hours.

   **TIP:** *The swirl recipe makes more than you need (the recipe won't work in smaller quantities). You can thin the leftovers with a little cream and use as a sundae topping, or you can enjoy it right off the spoon!*

**NOTE:** Ginger spread is a sweetened jarred (or canned) product that incorporates a potent gingery punch without any bitterness and won't cause the milk to curdle. And because it's completely smooth, there's no need to strain the final sauce. Look for it in the baking aisle of specialty grocery stores or online (see Sources on page 210).

### MAKE IT YOUR OWN

* Stir 2 tablespoons bourbon into the chilled base.
* Use store-bought dulce de leche in place of the ginger caramel swirl (you get what you pay for, so use a good one).

### SERVE IT WITH . . .

* Caramelized Banana Ice Cream (page 202), Salted Caramel Ice Cream (page 61), or Ricanelas Ice Cream (page 188) for Kris's favorite combo.

# BROWN SUGAR GRAHAM CRACKERS

Makes about twenty 3-inch crackers | Shown opposite as crackers and as a piecrust on page 40

These graham crackers are so much more flavorful than the boxed kind. They're a breeze to make, and once you try them you will wonder why you ever bought the commercial variety. They make a great topping crumbled onto ice cream, go into our favorite crust for the s'mores ice cream pie (see page 27), and are a fabulous after-school (or after-work) snack.

AT A GLANCE ········································································

CHILLING TIME: At least 2 hours                SHELF LIFE: 5 days for cookies, 1 week for crumbs

············································································

A heaping 1 1/2 cups (7 ounces) unbleached all-purpose flour, plus more as needed for rolling

1 1/3 cups (6 ounces) graham flour (see Note)

1 teaspoon baking soda

1/2 teaspoon kosher salt

1 cup (8 ounces) unsalted butter, at room temperature

2/3 cup packed dark brown sugar

3 tablespoons honey

3 tablespoons granulated sugar

1 tablespoon ground cinnamon

## MAKE THE DOUGH

1. In a large bowl, combine both flours, the baking soda, and salt and whisk to blend. Set aside.

2. In the bowl of a stand mixer with the paddle attachment, combine the butter, brown sugar, and honey and beat on medium-high speed until light and fluffy, about 2 minutes. Scrape down the sides of the bowl. Add the flour mixture and mix on low speed just until blended and the dough comes together, about 30 seconds.

3. Transfer the dough onto piece of plastic wrap, press into a 7-inch square, and wrap tightly. Refrigerate for at least 2 hours, or up to 5 days.

## TO MAKE COOKIES

4. Position racks in the top and bottom thirds of the oven and preheat the oven to 350°F. Line two large baking sheets with parchment paper or a nonstick mat.

5. On a lightly floured surface, roll out the dough to a 1/8-inch thickness and cut into squares (or any shape you want). Transfer to the baking sheet, spacing the cookies at least 3/4 inch apart. Gather any scraps, reroll, and cut out more cookies.

6. In a small bowl, combine the granulated sugar and cinnamon and sprinkle the mixture evenly over the cookies.

7. Bake the cookies for 10 minutes and then rotate the baking sheets. Bake for another 6 to 8 minutes, or until the cookies are dark golden brown and just firm to the touch. Let cool for a minute on the baking sheets, then transfer to a cooling rack. Let cool completely (they will crisp up as they cool).

Store in an airtight container.

Caramelized Banana Ice Cream (page 202) with Brown Sugar Graham Crackers and Caramel Sauce (page 71)

### TO MAKE CRUMBS FOR AN ICE CREAM PIE

4. Position racks in the top and bottom thirds of the oven and preheat the oven to 350°F. Line two baking sheets with parchment paper or nonstick mats.

5. Break the dough into walnut-sized lumps with your fingers and space them evenly on the baking sheets.

6. In a small bowl, combine the granulated sugar and cinnamon and sprinkle the mixture evenly over the dough. Bake for 10 minutes, then rotate the pans front to back and top to bottom. Continue to bake for another 10 to 15 minutes, or until the cookie pieces are golden brown and just firm to the touch.

7. Let cool completely on the baking sheets. Working in batches as necessary, transfer the cookie pieces to a food processor and pulse until they becomes a coarse meal. Store in an airtight container for up to a week at room temperature; freeze for longer storage.

> **NOTE:** Graham flour is similar to whole wheat flour but is ground differently and has a unique consistency as a result. You can substitute whole wheat flour if you like, but the texture will vary slightly.

# ALMOND TOFFEE

Makes 4 cups chopped toffee | Pictured on pages 102 and 130

What would we do without toffee? We love it and think it makes everything taste better (kind of like bacon!). We use it as a mix-in for ice cream, serve it as a topping (it's one of our most popular options), add it to cookies, top cupcakes with it, eat handfuls of it . . . pretty much anything goes!

## AT A GLANCE ·····································································

**SPECIAL EQUIPMENT:**
Candy thermometer

**COOLING TIME:**
1 hour

**SHELF LIFE:**
2 weeks or longer

·······································································

Nonstick cooking spray, for the pan (optional)

1 cup (8 ounces) unsalted butter

3/4 cup sugar

1/4 cup tapioca syrup or corn syrup

3 tablespoons water

1/2 teaspoon kosher salt

1 cup toasted slivered almonds (see page 114)

1. Line a large rimmed baking sheet with parchment paper or a nonstick mat, or spray it with nonstick cooking spray, and set aside.

2. Combine the butter, sugar, tapioca syrup, water, and salt in a medium saucepan and attach a candy thermometer. Put the pan over medium heat and cook, stirring frequently, until the mixture is dark amber and reaches 300°F, also known as the "hard crack" stage, 20 to 25 minutes.

   **TIP:** *Don't walk away from the pan, especially once it reaches around 250°F, when the mixture becomes more likely to burn.*

3. As soon as it reaches 300°F and the toffee is a deep brown color, take the pan off the heat, remove the thermometer, and stir in the almonds. Pour the mixture onto the prepared baking sheet and use a heatproof spatula to spread it out to a 1/4-inch thickness. (Be careful—it's extremely hot!)

4. Let cool for about an hour. If the top of the toffee sheet looks or feels a little greasy, just blot it off with a paper towel. Break or chop the toffee into chunks.

   This recipe may seem like it makes a lot of toffee, but it can be stored in an airtight container for a couple weeks.

---

**NOTE:** This is technically a candy recipe, not a caramel recipe, but the results are similar. And, just like when making caramel, timing is of the essence when making candy. For the best results, read through the entire recipe, measure out all of your ingredients, and set out the necessary equipment *before* you fire up the stove. A candy thermometer is essential.

**MAKE IT YOUR OWN**

※ Substitute any other nut for the almonds. We find, however, that slivered almonds provide the best textural contrast.

※ Add 1/4 teaspoon cayenne pepper to the sugar mixture. (Kris loves this spicy/sweet combo!)

---

# TOFFEE CHIP COOKIES

Makes about 40 cookies | Pictured on page 70

This is one of those recipes that came about as a happy accident. We had been tinkering with our pecan toffee recipe but hadn't quite gotten it right. Rather than toss out the not-quite-perfect outcome, we chopped the toffee and added it to a batch of cookie dough. The result was the ideal union of a candy and a cookie. Toffee Chip Cookies have become even more popular than our Chocolate Chip Cookies!

## AT A GLANCE

**CHILLING TIME:** 2 hours or up to overnight

**SHELF LIFE:** 5 days

---

$2^2/3$ cups (12 ounces) unbleached
    all-purpose flour

1 teaspoon baking powder

$1/2$ teaspoon kosher salt

$1/4$ teaspoon baking soda

$3/4$ cup (6 ounces) unsalted butter,
    at room temperature

$3/4$ cup granulated sugar

$3/4$ cup packed light or dark brown sugar

3 large eggs

$1^1/2$ teaspoons pure vanilla extract

2 cups coarsely chopped Almond Toffee
    (opposite)

$3^1/2$ ounces bittersweet chocolate (60% to
    65% cacao; see Note), coarsely chopped
    (about 1 cup)

> **TIP:** *If you leave your toffee in larger pieces, the toffee will melt in little pockets, producing a very lacy and crunchy cookie.*

> **NOTE:** We prefer to use hand-chopped chocolate, but chocolate chips can easily be substituted. However, bittersweet chocolate is preferable to semisweet here, as the toffee already contributes a lot of sweetness and bittersweet chocolate provides a nice contrast.

1. In a medium bowl, combine the flour, baking powder, salt, and baking soda and whisk to combine. Set aside.

2. In the bowl of a stand mixer with the paddle attachment, combine the butter and both sugars. Mix on medium-high speed until light in color and fluffy, about 2 minutes. Scrape down the bowl and, with the motor running, add the eggs one at a time, completely mixing in each egg before adding the next. Scrape down the bowl, add the vanilla, and mix until blended, about 15 seconds. Add the toffee and chocolate and mix on low speed just until blended. Add the flour mixture and mix on low speed just until the dough comes together, about 15 seconds.

3. Cover the bowl with plastic wrap and chill until the dough is firm, at least 2 hours or up to overnight.

4. When you're ready to bake, position racks in the top and bottom thirds of the oven and preheat the oven to 350°F. Line two baking sheets with parchment paper or nonstick mats.

CONTINUED

5. Scoop up 2 tablespoons of dough (we use a 1-ounce ice cream scoop) and form the dough into a ball. Repeat until all the dough has been shaped. Place the balls 2½ inches apart on the baking sheets. Flatten the balls slightly with the palm of your hand so that they're about ½ inch thick.

6. Bake for 6 minutes, then rotate the baking sheets top to bottom and front to back. Continue to bake until the cookies are golden on the edges and just barely set in the center, 6 to 7 minutes longer.

7. Let the cookies cool for a minute on the baking sheets, then transfer to a rack and let cool completely. Bake the remaining dough balls. Store the cookies in an airtight container.

**TIP:** *If you do not want to bake all the cookies at once, scoop the cookie dough into balls and arrange in a single layer on a baking sheet. Freeze until solid, then transfer to a zip-top bag and keep in the freezer until the desire for a warm cookie calls.*

# CARAMEL SAUCE

Makes about 1¼ cups | Pictured on pages 67 and 194

This sauce is very simple but very delicious. We always take our caramel to that dark mahogany color, which produces a fairly robust, slightly bitter caramel flavor. If you prefer something a little tamer, just add the cream when the sugar is a lighter shade. After a few tries you will find the color of caramel that is perfect for your taste.

This sauce is best served just warm, poured over your favorite ice cream or any other dessert. It's great with apple pie, between layers of chocolate cake, or drizzled on a sundae.

## AT A GLANCE

TECHNIQUES: Caramel (page 56)　　COOLING TIME: About 1 hour　　SHELF LIFE: 2 weeks

---

3/4 cup heavy cream, at room temperature
1 cup sugar
1/4 teaspoon kosher salt

1. Set the cream by the stove so it's at hand when you need it. Put 2 tablespoons of the sugar in a heavy nonreactive saucepan and put the pan over medium-high heat. When the sugar is melted around the edges and starts turn amber in places (about 2 minutes), stir the mixture gently and add another 2 tablespoons sugar to the pan.

2. Continue to add the remaining sugar 2 tablespoons at a time, stirring as needed and allowing most of the sugar to melt before you add more. Watch carefully as the sugar darkens, stirring gently to help it melt evenly.

3. When the caramel becomes a dark mahogany color, remove the pan from the heat and immediately but slowly pour the cream into the pan. (The mixture will steam and bubble up, so wear oven mitts and be very careful to avoid splatters and steam burns.) When the bubbling subsides, gently stir to completely blend the cream into the caramel. If you have lumps of hardened caramel in your pan, simply put the pan over low heat and stir until the caramel is melted.

4. Stir in the salt and let cool until just warm. (The sauce will stay rippin' hot for quite a while, so resist the urge to lick the spoon.) If not using within a few hours, transfer to a container and refrigerate. Rewarm before using.

### MAKE IT YOUR OWN

* Create another layer of flavor by replacing up to 1/4 cup of the cream with another liquid once the caramel is made and still warm. Try bourbon (a personal favorite of ours), apple juice, coffee, or calvados (a French apple brandy).

# CHOCOLATE

UNLESS YOU'VE WORKED IN A BAKERY, you may not realize just how much manual labor goes into making ice cream and baked goods. This truth is perhaps best exemplified by chocolate. We get our chocolate in 11-pound blocks, which have to be chopped into small pieces before they can be used in our recipes. Our hardworking prep cooks are responsible for this task, chopping more than 220 pounds of chocolate every week! The guys demonstrate a healthy amount of competition, each one boasting to be the fastest or most efficient, and each with his own unique technique. Selvin likes to think he's the best and tries to indoctrinate everyone with his method of breaking the block into smaller chunks before chopping each individually. Some of the other guys rest the slab on its side, nestle the short end under their arms, and use a knife to shave down the other side. It helps to have a little bit of a gut for that technique; it acts as a cushion against the hard block of chocolate (like those pictured on page 72).

## BUYING AND USING CHOCOLATE

It's very easy to spend a lot of money on a relatively small quantity of chocolate. To a certain extent, spending more will get you a better product. However, for baking and confectionary purposes (like making ice cream), there is a point of diminishing returns as far as chocolate goes. The best rule of thumb is to use chocolate that is of good quality but is not outrageously expensive. At the Creamery, we use several different brands of chocolate, but the one we use most often is one you might find at your grocery store: Callebaut, a brand that is the favorite of many a pastry chef.

Far more important than choosing the brand of chocolate is using the correct type of chocolate for the recipe. By this we mean matching the cacao percentage specified in the recipe. This number, which appears prominently on the label of most high-quality chocolates, indicates the proportion of cacao solids relative to the other ingredients (which are almost always sugar, cocoa butter, vanilla, and lecithin, an emulsifier). The higher the percentage of cacao, the less sugar and fat there is in the chocolate. This is important not just for flavor but also for the chemistry of the recipe itself. Using a very dark chocolate instead of the prescribed semisweet in a recipe can produce results that differ in texture, flavor, and consistency from those that were intended.

Unfortunately, many recipes in other books don't specify the type of chocolate they want you to use, and, on top of that, chocolate labels can be confusing and inconsistent from one brand to the next. To help clarify things, here's a brief rundown of the basic categories of chocolate, and some brands that we like of each type.

**Unsweetened** chocolate contains cacao solids and cocoa butter but no sugar. Using

unsweetened chocolate gives the baker more control over how much sugar goes into a recipe and more control over what kind of sweetener to use (for instance, you might want to use honey instead of sugar). We use Callebaut for our unsweetened chocolate but Valrhona is another good choice.

**Bittersweet** chocolate is basically unsweetened chocolate with sugar, lecithin, and vanilla incorporated into the mix. Sugar makes the chocolate tastier (take a nibble of unsweetened chocolate if you don't believe us) and makes it a good multipurpose chocolate, suitable for melting, dipping, and eating. Most bittersweet chocolate falls in the 52 percent to 65 percent cacao range, although it can go much higher. We actually prefer to use bittersweet chocolate in the middle of the range—around 60 percent—because it strikes a good balance of sweetness and chocolate flavor. Higher percentages can make the overall flavor of a recipe too bitter. We use Callebaut bittersweet chocolate. Some other good choices include Valrhona, El Rey, and Madécasse. The recipes in this book using

bittersweet chocolate were developed with 52 percent to 60 percent chocolate.

**Semisweet** chocolate generally refers to chocolate that has a fairly high percentage of sugar (and therefore a fairly low percent of cacao). Good ole chocolate chips are the most common form of semisweet chocolate.

**Milk** chocolate features the addition of—you guessed it—milk for a creamier flavor and more meltable consistency. It usually has a fairly high sugar content as well. We use Callebaut milk chocolate but other good options include El Rey and Madécasse.

**White** chocolate is made of cocoa butter, sugar, vanilla, and lecithin but contains no cocoa solids (and for this reason it is not technically chocolate). Most white chocolate is highly processed, including an unsavory-sounding deodorization step. The white chocolate that we use, El Rey, is not deodorized and has a nice malty flavor to it. We consider it to be the best around. Other excellent choices are Callebaut and Valrhona.

The best-value chocolate (that is, the best quality for the price, especially for baking and such) is usually stocked in the cheese section of better grocery stores. These are the big blocks of chocolate that the store breaks up into 1-pound blocks, wraps, and weighs for individual sale. (Most of the time it's Callebaut or Valrhona chocolate, both solid choices.) You'll pay less per pound by buying it like this, and it will stay fresher longer because they have less surface area compared to smaller bars or chips.

**TIP:** *But what about chips? They're fine to use in recipes as along as they contain the correct percentage of cacao (but, unfortunately, most chips are not labeled with this information). They do have a shorter shelf life because they have more surface area compared to a bar of chocolate.*

Foreground: Chocolate Ice Cream (page 78)
with Balsamic Strawberry Ice Cream (page 138);
background: Mint Chip Ice Cream (page 182)

Heat and humidity are chocolate's main enemies, and it also has a tendency to absorb nearby odors. So for best results, keep chocolate tightly wrapped in plastic wrap and store it in a cool, dark place such as a cabinet. The refrigerator is too humid and it has too many other odors swirling about, so don't store it there . . . and don't put it in the freezer, either! When stored properly, chocolate will stay good for at least a year.

For best results, chop the chocolate relatively close to the time you plan to use it. Up to a week or so would be fine, but any more than that and the extra surface area can invite bloom and the absorption of other odors.

Chopping chocolate can be a little laborious, but the right tools and techniques can make it easier (just ask our prep cooks). An offset serrated knife (the kind where the blade hangs a few inches below the handle) gives you more leverage as you chop. And if you're chopping a particularly thick block, it's easier if you attack the corners of the block rather than going along a straight side.

Bloom is that white powdery substance you sometimes see on the surface of a bar of chocolate. This harmless condition is an indicator that the chocolate is "going out of temper"—in other words, the cocoa butter is separating out. Chocolate that has a little surface bloom is usually fine to use in recipes, especially if you're going to melt the chocolate anyway. However, if you break the chocolate apart and see bloom all the way through, you're probably better off getting fresh supplies.

## COCOA POWDER

Cocoa powder is made solely from cacao solids, and contains none of the cocoa butter, sugar, vanilla, or lecithin you'd get in a bar of chocolate. Because cocoa powder is pure cacao, we tend to use it in recipes where we want an intense chocolaty flavor. Our chocolate ice cream is a good example; the fat in the cream and milk are going to dilute the chocolate somewhat anyway, so using pure cacao (versus a melted bar of chocolate) helps keep the chocolate flavor as concentrated as possible.

All cocoa powder falls into one of two categories: natural or Dutch-processed. **Natural cocoa powder** is relatively self-explanatory; the cacao solids are extracted from the processed cocoa beans and allowed to dry before being ground into powder. **Dutch-processed cocoa** undergoes an additional step of alkalization, which produces cocoa powder that is very dark brown in color and less acidic than its natural cousin. It also has a markedly different flavor—it's richer and more chocolaty.

The differing pH levels of the two types of cocoa also changes the way it behaves in baking recipes, especially those using acid-dependent leaveners like baking soda. For this reason we don't recommend substituting natural and Dutch-processed cocoa powder for one another in recipes. You may be disappointed by a sunken cake or other such mishaps.

Nearly all of our recipes were developed using Dutch-processed cocoa powder. If you only have the natural kind, you can use the following formula to approximate it: 3 tablespoons Dutch-processed cocoa powder = 3 tablespoons natural cocoa powder + $\frac{1}{8}$ teaspoon baking soda.

# CHOCOLATE ICE CREAM

Makes about 1 quart | Pictured as an ice cream sandwich on page 209

As we were developing the recipes for this book, we made two different batches of our chocolate ice cream, one using natural cocoa powder and one using Dutch-processed. The results were astounding. The version made with Dutch cocoa was dark, intense, and trufflelike in its flavor, while the natural version seemed more like milk chocolate ice cream. The results are addictive either way.

## AT A GLANCE

| TECHNIQUE: | SPECIAL EQUIPMENT: | CHILLING TIME: | SHELF LIFE: |
|---|---|---|---|
| Ice cream (page 12) | Ice cream machine | 2 hours or overnight | 1 week |

5 large egg yolks

3/4 cup sugar

1/4 cup Dutch-processed or natural cocoa powder, measured then sifted (see headnote)

1 cup 1% or 2% milk

1 3/4 cups heavy cream

1/4 teaspoon kosher salt

1 teaspoon pure vanilla extract

### MAKE IT YOUR OWN

❊ Fold in chopped toasted hazelnuts (see page 114) for a Nutella-like effect.

❊ Add a swirl of Fudge Ripple (page 122) for chocolate-on-chocolate action.

### SERVE IT WITH . . .

❊ Blackberry Ice Cream (page 143) or Orange-Cardamom Ice Cream (page 158)

## MAKE THE BASE

1. In a medium heatproof bowl, whisk the yolks just to break them up, then whisk in half of the sugar (6 tablespoons). Set aside.

2. In a heavy nonreactive saucepan, combine the cocoa powder with the remaining sugar (6 tablespoons). Whisk in about 1/4 cup of the milk to make a paste, adding a little more of the milk as needed to make it smooth and uniform. (If you add the milk all at once, the cocoa will be lumpy.) Whisk in the remaining milk, the cream, and salt and put the pan over medium-high heat. When the mixture approaches a bare simmer, reduce the heat to medium.

3. Carefully scoop out about 1/2 cup of the hot cream mixture and, whisking the eggs constantly, add the cream to the bowl with the egg yolks. Repeat, adding another 1/2 cup of the hot cream to the bowl with the yolks. Using a heatproof rubber spatula, stir the

cream in the saucepan as you slowly pour the egg-and-cream mixture from the bowl into the pan.

4. Cook the mixture carefully over medium heat, stirring constantly, until it is thickened, coats the back of a spatula, and holds a clear path when you run your finger across the spatula, 1 to 2 minutes longer.

5. Strain the base through a fine-mesh strainer into a clean container. Set the container into an ice-water bath, wash your spatula, and use it to stir the base occasionally until it is cool. Remove the container from the ice-water bath, cover with plastic wrap, and refrigerate the base for at least 2 hours or overnight.

### FREEZE THE ICE CREAM

6. Add the vanilla to the base and stir until blended.

7. Freeze in your ice cream machine according to the manufacturer's instructions. While the ice cream is churning, put the container you'll use to store the ice cream into the freezer. Enjoy right away or, for a firmer ice cream, transfer to the chilled container and freeze for at least 4 hours.

## SAM'S SUNDAE

One of the most popular sundaes at the Creamery was invented by (and named after) Anne's husband, Sam. It features Chocolate Ice Cream topped with bergamot olive oil, a sprinkle of Maldon sea salt, and a dollop of whipped cream. The citrusy olive oil is a perfectly luxurious match for the chocolate, and the salt leaves your taste buds wanting more.

# CHAI-SPICED MILK CHOCOLATE ICE CREAM

Makes about 1 quart

Imagine mixing hot chocolate with chai tea and then churning it into ice cream. This recipe gives you just that! It's a sophisticated mixture of warm, wintry, exotic spices tempered by creamy milk chocolate. It was inspired by a "milk chocolate masala" candy bar that Kris bought during her travels. As she tasted it with her husband, Nate, she immediately realized how good it would be as an ice cream.

## AT A GLANCE

TECHNIQUE:
Ice cream (page 12)

SPECIAL EQUIPMENT:
Ice cream machine

CHILLING TIME: 30 minutes
to infuse the cream,
2 1/2 hours or overnight
to chill the base

SHELF LIFE:
1 week

15 whole black peppercorns

10 whole cloves

7 green cardamom pods

2 cinnamon sticks

2 whole star anise

1 1/4 cups heavy cream

1 cup 1% or 2% milk

1/4 cup sugar

1/4 teaspoon kosher salt

5 large egg yolks

6 ounces milk chocolate, finely chopped
(about 1 1/4 cups)

### TOAST THE SPICES

1. Combine the peppercorns, cloves, cardamom, cinnamon, and star anise in a medium nonreactive saucepan and put the pan over medium-high heat. Toast, stirring frequently, until the spices are aromatic, 2 to 3 minutes.

2. Add the cream, milk, sugar, and salt and increase the heat to medium-high. When the mixture just begins to bubble around the edges, remove from the heat and cover the pan. Let steep for about 30 minutes, or until the cream has taken on a distinct chailike flavor. (Stir it occasionally and taste it to monitor the progress.)

### MAKE THE BASE

3. In a medium heatproof bowl, whisk the yolks just to break them up and set aside. Put the chopped chocolate in another medium heatproof bowl and set that aside as well.

4. Put the pan of infused cream over medium-high heat. When the mixture approaches a bare simmer, reduce the heat to medium.

5. Carefully scoop out about ½ cup of the hot cream mixture and, whisking the eggs constantly, add the cream to the bowl with the egg yolks. Repeat, adding another ½ cup of the hot cream to the bowl with the yolks. Using a heatproof rubber spatula, stir the cream in the saucepan as you slowly pour the egg-and-cream mixture from the bowl into the pan.

6. Cook the mixture carefully over medium heat, stirring constantly, until it is thickened, coats the back of a spatula, and holds a clear path when you run your finger across the spatula, 1 to 2 minutes longer.

7. Pour the hot cream mixture into the bowl of chopped chocolate, wash your whisk, and whisk until smooth.

8. Strain the base through a fine-mesh strainer into a clean container. Set the container into an ice-water bath, wash your spatula, and use it to stir the base occasionally until it is cool. Remove the container from the ice-water bath, cover with plastic wrap, and refrigerate the base for at least 2 hours or overnight.

## FREEZE THE ICE CREAM

9. Freeze in your ice cream machine according to the manufacturer's instructions. While the ice cream is churning, put the container you'll use to store the ice cream into the freezer. Enjoy right away or, for a firmer ice cream, transfer to the chilled container and freeze for at least 4 hours.

### MAKE IT YOUR OWN
✳ Add finely chopped milk chocolate or toasted chopped cashews or macadamia nuts (see page 114) in the last minute or so of churning.

### SERVE IT WITH . . .
✳ Pistachio Ice Cream (page 119) or Cheesecake Ice Cream (page 41)

# MALTED MILK CHOCOLATE ICE CREAM
## with BITTERSWEET CHOCOLATE CHIPS

Makes about 1 quart

Anne says, "This is my all-time favorite ice cream. I first had it in 1991, when I was working for pastry chef Patrick DeLessio at the Stanford Court Hotel in San Francisco. Patrick was inspired by the wonderful malted ice cream flavors created by Steve Herrell of Herrell's Ice Cream in Northampton, Massachusetts. The malted milk powder contributes an almost earthy sweetness to the milk chocolate ice cream base. Chopped bittersweet chocolate provides textural contrast and a deeper chocolate flavor."

## AT A GLANCE

| TECHNIQUE: | SPECIAL EQUIPMENT: | CHILLING TIME: | SHELF LIFE: |
|---|---|---|---|
| Ice cream (page 12) | Ice cream machine | 2 hours or overnight | 1 week |

6 large egg yolks

6 ounces milk chocolate, finely chopped (about 1¼ cups)

1¾ cups heavy cream

1 cup 1% or 2% milk

¾ cup malted milk powder (Carnation or a similar product)

½ teaspoon kosher salt

4 ounces bittersweet chocolate (52% to 60% cacao), finely chopped (scant 1 cup)

### MAKE THE BASE

1. In a medium heatproof bowl, whisk the yolks just to break them up. Put the chopped milk chocolate in another medium heatproof bowl and set both bowls aside.

2. In a heavy nonreactive saucepan, whisk together the cream, milk, malted milk powder, and salt and put the pan over medium-high heat. When the mixture approaches a bare simmer, reduce the heat to medium.

3. Carefully scoop out about ½ cup of the hot cream mixture and, whisking the eggs constantly, add the cream to the bowl with the egg yolks. Repeat, adding another ½ cup of the hot cream to the bowl with the yolks. Using a heatproof rubber spatula, stir the cream in the saucepan as you slowly pour the egg-and-cream mixture from the bowl into the pan.

4. Cook the mixture carefully over medium heat, stirring constantly, until it is thickened, coats the back of a spatula, and holds a clear path when you run your finger across the spatula, 1 to 2 minutes longer.

5. Pour the hot cream mixture into the bowl of chopped chocolate, wash your whisk, and whisk until smooth.

6. Strain the base through a fine-mesh strainer into a clean container. Set the container

into an ice-water bath, wash your spatula, and use it to stir the base occasionally until it is cool. Remove the container from the ice-water bath, cover with plastic wrap, and refrigerate the base for at least 2 hours or overnight.

FREEZE THE ICE CREAM

7. Freeze in your ice cream machine according to the manufacturer's instructions. While the ice cream is churning, put the container you'll use to store the ice cream into the freezer. Add the chopped bittersweet chocolate in the last minute or so of churning, or fold it in by hand after the ice cream comes out of the machine. Enjoy right away or, for a firmer ice cream, transfer to the chilled container and freeze for at least 4 hours.

**MAKE IT YOUR OWN**

❋ Instead of using bittersweet chocolate, try adding chopped toasted nuts (cashews are especially good; see page 114), chopped Almond Toffee (page 68), or a swirl of Fudge Ripple (page 122).

**SERVE IT WITH . . .**

❋ Crème Fraîche Ice Cream (page 38) or Peanut Butter Fudge Swirl Ice Cream (page 123)

❋ A sprinkle of chopped Almond Toffee (page 68)

# COOKIES *and* CREAM ICE CREAM

Makes about 1¼ quarts | Pictured on page 97

Along with Mint Chip Ice Cream (page 182), this is one of the most popular flavors among our younger guests. It's also one of the only recipes for which we *don't* make the mix-in ingredient from scratch. The truth is, it's hard to improve on the perfection of Newman-O's, and so that's what we use. You can use them, too, or try any other cookie you like. The Dark Chocolate Cookies on page 90 are especially good!

## AT A GLANCE

| TECHNIQUE: | SPECIAL EQUIPMENT: | CHILLING TIME: | SHELF LIFE: |
|---|---|---|---|
| Ice cream (page 12) | Ice cream machine | 2 hours or overnight | 1 week |

5 large egg yolks

½ cup sugar

1¾ cups heavy cream

¾ cup 1% or 2% milk

¼ teaspoon kosher salt

2 teaspoons pure vanilla extract

1¼ cups chopped chocolate cookies (in pieces ¼ inch or larger)

### MAKE THE BASE

1. In a medium heatproof bowl, whisk the yolks just to break them up, then whisk in half of the sugar (¼ cup). Set aside.

2. In a heavy nonreactive saucepan, stir together the cream, milk, salt, and the remaining sugar (¼ cup) and put the pan over medium-high heat. When the mixture approaches a bare simmer, reduce the heat to medium.

3. Carefully scoop out about ½ cup of the hot cream mixture and, whisking the eggs constantly, add the cream to the bowl with the egg yolks. Repeat, adding another ½ cup of the hot cream to the bowl with the yolks. Using a heatproof rubber spatula, stir the cream in the saucepan as you slowly pour the egg-and-cream mixture from the bowl into the pan.

4. Cook the mixture carefully over medium heat, stirring constantly, until it is thickened, coats the back of a spatula, and holds a clear path when you run your finger across the spatula, 1 to 2 minutes longer.

5. Strain the base through a fine-mesh strainer into a clean container. Set the container into an ice-water bath, wash your spatula, and use it to stir the base occasionally until it is cool. Remove the container from the ice-water bath, cover with plastic wrap, and refrigerate the base for at least 2 hours or overnight.

FREEZE THE ICE CREAM

6. Freeze in your ice cream machine according to the manufacturer's instructions. While the ice cream is churning, put the container you'll use to store the ice cream into the freezer. Add the chopped cookies in the last minute or so of churning, or fold them in by hand after the ice cream comes out of the machine. Enjoy right away or, for a firmer ice cream, transfer to the chilled container and freeze for at least 4 hours.

**SERVE IT WITH . . .**
* Mint Chip Ice Cream (page 182)—a kid's dream combo!
* Ricanelas Ice Cream (page 188)—we call this combo with two flavors that feature chopped cookies "The Cookie Monster."

# BROWNIES

Makes nine 3-inch-square brownies

These brownies were one of the first recipes we made for sale at Bi-Rite Market, and they have continued to be a mainstay in our lineup over the years. We started with a borrowed recipe (the source now forgotten), but we tweaked it by upping the amount of unsweetened chocolate for a more intense flavor. The resulting recipe, we think, has it all: the brownies are rich and dark, and you can make them in no time.

We use these as the base for our brownie sundae, which is topped with vanilla ice cream, chocolate and caramel sauces, whipped cream, and spiced pecans. It's over the top in the best way possible!

## AT A GLANCE

COOLING TIME: About 1 hour

SHELF LIFE: 1 week

1 cup (4$^1$/$_2$ ounces) unbleached all-purpose flour

1 teaspoon baking powder

1 teaspoon kosher salt

$^1$/$_2$ cup (4 ounces) unsalted butter, cut into 1-inch pieces, plus more for the pan

4 ounces unsweetened chocolate, coarsely chopped (1 cup)

2 ounces bittersweet chocolate (preferably about 52% cacao), coarsely chopped ($^1$/$_2$ cup)

1$^3$/$_4$ cups sugar

4 large eggs

1. Position a rack in the center of the oven and preheat the oven to 350°F. Butter a 9-inch square baking pan and line the bottom with parchment paper. In a small bowl, whisk together the flour, baking powder, and salt and set aside.

2. Put 1 inch of water in the bottom of a double boiler or medium saucepan and bring to a simmer over medium-high heat.

CONTINUED

If you are using a gas stove, make sure the flames are not coming up around the pan, which can cause the chocolate to scorch.

In the top of the double boiler or in a medium heatproof bowl, combine the butter and both chocolates. Put the pan or bowl over but not touching the simmering water. Whisk frequently until the chocolates are melted and completely smooth, about 4 minutes. Remove from the heat. If using a double boiler, transfer the chocolate to a medium bowl.

3. Add the sugar to the chocolate and stir until blended. Then add the eggs one at a time, completely blending in each one before adding the next. Add the flour mixture all at once and mix just until blended. (If you prefer, you can mix this batter in a stand mixer with the paddle attachment.) Transfer to the prepared pan and spread to an even thickness.

4. Bake until a toothpick inserted in the center of the brownies comes out with a few moist crumbs clinging to it, 25 to 30 minutes. Let cool completely in the pan before cutting into squares.

Store the brownies in an airtight container at room temperature.

**MAKE IT YOUR OWN**

❈ Add ½ cup chopped toasted walnuts, pecans, or almonds (see page 114) to the batter.

**TIP:** There's a trick to cutting brownies so that they are perfect squares with clean edges. First, run a knife around the edge of the pan and invert the pan onto a cutting board. (If the brownies don't release on their own, give the pan a good whack onto the board.) Lift off the pan, peel off the parchment, and carefully turn the slab right side up (for more stability, put another cutting board on top of the brownies and hold both boards together as you flip them over). Use a ruler and a knife to measure and lightly mark each point where you plan to cut. Then lay the ruler across the top of the slab to connect two of the opposing points. Repeat with each set of opposing guide marks to make sure they are evenly spaced. When you're ready to make the first cut, hold the ruler in place, line your knife up against the ruler, and cut straight down (if you make a sawing motion, the crumbs will stick and make ragged edges). Clean off the knife with a damp kitchen towel or rinse it under warm water, dry it off, and make your next cut.

# CHOCOLATE CHIP COOKIES

Makes about 4 dozen cookies

We've been making these cookies ever since our days at the restaurant 42 Degrees. The secret is in using chopped bittersweet chocolate, which gives you more variety in size and shape compared to chips; the bigger chunks create the classic pockets of chocolate, and the tiny shards permeate the dough itself, creating a sort of chocolate-on-chocolate effect.

## AT A GLANCE

CHILLING TIME: At least 2 hours or up to overnight          SHELF LIFE: 5 days

2$1/2$ cups (11$1/4$ ounces) unbleached all-purpose flour

1 teaspoon kosher salt

1 teaspoon baking soda

1 cup (8 ounces) unsalted butter, at room temperature

$3/4$ cups granulated sugar

$3/4$ cups packed brown sugar, preferably dark

2 large eggs

$3/4$ teaspoon pure vanilla extract

9 ounces bittersweet chocolate (52% to 60% cacao), chopped, with the largest pieces the size of chocolate chips (scant 2 cups)

1. In a medium bowl, whisk together the flour, salt, and baking soda and set aside.

2. In the bowl of a stand mixer with the paddle attachment, combine the butter and both sugars. Mix on medium-high speed until lightened in color and fluffy, about 2 minutes. With the motor running, add the eggs one at a time, blending thoroughly after each addition, then add the vanilla.

    Scrape down the bowl, add the chocolate, and mix on low speed until combined. Add the flour mixture and mix on low speed just until the dough comes together, about 15 seconds.

3. Cover the bowl with plastic wrap and refrigerate until the dough is firm, at least 2 hours or up to overnight.

4. When you're ready to bake, position racks in the top and bottom thirds of the oven and preheat the oven to 350°F. Line two baking sheets with parchment paper or nonstick mats.

5. Scoop up 2 tablespoons of dough (we use a 1-ounce ice cream scoop) and form the dough into a ball. Repeat until all the dough has been shaped. Place the balls 2$1/2$ inches apart on the baking sheets. Flatten the balls slightly with the palm of your hand so that they're about $1/2$ inch thick.

6. Bake for 7 minutes, then rotate the baking sheets top to bottom and front to back. Continue to bake until the cookies are golden brown, 7 to 9 minutes longer.

    Let the cookies cool for a minute or two on the baking sheets, then transfer to a rack and let cool completely. Repeat with the remaining dough. Store in an airtight container.

# CHOCOLATE MIDNIGHT CAKE

Makes one 8-inch round cake (enough for 1 ice cream cake) or 16 cupcakes | Shown opposite and as an ice cream cake on page 102

We have Mary Cech, pastry chef at San Francisco's famed (and now-closed) Cypress Club, to thank for this versatile recipe. It's best known among our guests as a layer cake topped with cream cheese frosting, but we also use it as the base for ice cream cakes and cupcakes. The crumb is dark—almost black—and so moist that we don't recommend soaking it with syrups or sauces. As an added bonus, the extra moisture gives it an excellent shelf life.

## AT A GLANCE

SPECIAL EQUIPMENT: One round cake pan, 8 inches in diameter and 2 inches deep, or two standard muffin pans

COOLING TIME:
About 1 hour

SHELF LIFE:
5 days

---

Nonstick cooking spray or unsalted butter, for the pans

1$^1$/$_2$ cups sugar

$^3$/$_4$ cup (3$^1$/$_2$ ounces) unbleached all-purpose flour

$^3$/$_4$ cup (3$^1$/$_2$ ounces) cake flour

1$^3$/$_4$ ounces ($^1$/$_2$ cup) Dutch-processed cocoa powder, measured then sifted

1 teaspoon baking soda

$^1$/$_2$ teaspoon kosher salt

1$^1$/$_2$ cups boiling water

2 large eggs

$^1$/$_2$ cup canola or other neutral-flavored oil

1. Position racks in the upper third and lower third of the oven and preheat the oven to 350°F. If making a cake, spray or butter a round cake pan, 8 inches in diameter by 2 inches deep, and line the bottom with parchment paper. If making cupcakes, line sixteen cups of two standard muffin pans with paper or foil liners.

2. In a mixing bowl, whisk together the sugar, both flours, the cocoa, baking soda, and salt. Gradually whisk the boiling water into the flour, adding about $^1$/$_2$ cup of the water at a time, until all the water is added and you have a smooth, thick batter. Whisk in the eggs one at a time, blending well after each addition, then whisk in the oil. You should have a very thin but smooth batter.

3. Pour the batter into the cake pan or divide among the muffin cups. Bake until the cake springs back to a light touch and a toothpick inserted into the center comes out clean, 50 to 55 minutes for the cake and about 25 minutes for cupcakes.

4. Let the cake cool in the pan for 30 minutes, then invert onto a wire rack. Remove the parchment and let cool completely. Let the cupcakes cool in the pans for 30 minutes before transferring onto a wire rack, then let cool completely.

> **SERVE IT WITH . . .**
> ❊ Cheesecake Ice Cream (page 41) and Chocolate Glaze (page 94) for a frozen version of our popular layer cake
> ❊ Berry Compote (page 148) or Raspberry Swirl Sauce (page 142)

Chocolate Midnight Cakes with Vanilla
Buttercream Frosting (page 49)

# DARK CHOCOLATE COOKIES

Makes about 50 cookies | Pictured as an ice cream sandwich on page 209 and as piecrust on page 97

Just like our Chocolate Midnight Cake (page 88), these cookies are so dark as to be almost black. Dark Chocolate Cookies are a wonderful cookie for an ice cream sandwich, crisp but still a little chewy, and they pair nicely with many flavors.

## AT A GLANCE

CHILLING TIME: At least 2 hours or up to overnight     SHELF LIFE: 5 days

2²/3 cups (12 ounces) unbleached all-purpose flour

8 ounces (2 cups) Dutch-processed cocoa powder, measured then sifted

4¹/2 teaspoons baking soda

¹/2 teaspoon kosher salt

1³/4 cups plus 2 tablespoons (15 ounces) unsalted butter, at room temperature

2 cups granulated sugar

1 cup packed light or dark brown sugar

3 large eggs

1. In a medium bowl, whisk together the flour, cocoa powder, baking soda, and salt and set aside.

2. In the bowl of a stand mixer with the paddle attachment, combine the butter and both sugars. Mix on medium-high speed until lightened in color and fluffy, about 2 minutes. Scrape down the bowl and, with the motor running, add the eggs one at a time, completely mixing in each egg before adding the next.

   Scrape down the sides of the bowl, add the flour mixture, and mix on low speed just until the dough comes together, about 30 seconds.

3. Cover the bowl with plastic wrap and chill until the dough is firm, at least 2 hours or up to overnight.

4. When you're ready to bake, position racks in the top and bottom thirds of the oven and preheat the oven to 350°F. Line two baking sheets with parchment paper or nonstick mats.

   Scoop up 2 tablespoons of dough (we use a 1-ounce ice cream scoop) and form the dough into a ball. Repeat until all the dough has been shaped. Place the balls 2¹/2 inches apart on the baking sheets. Flatten the balls slightly with the palm of your hand so that they're about ¹/2 inch thick.

5. Bake for 5 minutes, and then rotate the baking sheets top to bottom and front to back. Continued to bake until the cookies are slightly cracked on the surface and feel dry and slightly firm in the center, 5 to 6 minutes longer. (If they feel airy, like a soufflé, they're not ready.)

   Let cool for a minute on the baking sheets, then transfer to a rack. Bake the remaining dough balls. Let cool completely and then store in an airtight container.

### MAKE IT YOUR OWN

❋ Add 1 teaspoon peppermint extract after adding the eggs.
❋ Add 2 cups coarsely chopped white chocolate after mixing in the flour.

# CHOCOLATE SHORTBREAD

Makes about 28 two-inch cookies, one 9- or 10-inch tart crust, or 4 cups of crumbs

We use this recipe to make crusts for ice cream pies as well as for banana cream and other cream pies at the market. In addition to using the crushed crumbs to make a piecrust and for layering them in desserts, you can also roll out the dough to make shortbread cookies or a tart crust.

## AT A GLANCE

**CHILLING TIME:** 2 hours or up to overnight for cookies or tart crust

**SHELF LIFE:** 10 days for cookies, 2 weeks for crumbs

1 cup (8 ounces) cold unsalted butter, cut into $^1/_2$-inch cubes

$1^1/_2$ cups ($6^3/_4$ ounces) unbleached all-purpose flour, more for dusting

1 cup ($5^1/_3$ ounces) powdered sugar, measured then sifted

$1^3/_4$ ounces ($^1/_2$ cup) Dutch-processed cocoa powder, measured then sifted

$^1/_2$ teaspoon kosher salt

$^1/_2$ teaspoon pure vanilla extract

### MAKE THE DOUGH

1. Combine all of the ingredients in the bowl of a stand mixer with the paddle attachment. Mix on low speed at first, and then increase to medium-low speed and continue mixing until the dough is smooth and just comes together in a solid mass, $1^1/_2$ to 2 minutes.

### TO MAKE COOKIES

2. Turn the dough out onto a piece of plastic wrap and shape into a disk 1 inch thick.

CONTINUED

Wrap in the plastic wrap and refrigerate until firm, 1 to 2 hours or up to overnight.

3. When you're ready to bake, position racks in the top and bottom thirds of the oven and preheat the oven to 350°F. Line two baking sheets with parchment paper or nonstick mats.

4. On a lightly floured surface, roll the dough to ¼-inch thickness (or slightly thicker or thinner, if you like). Using a cookie cutter (or a knife for free-form shapes), cut out cookies from the dough. If you use a cutter, gather and reroll the scraps up to two more times; any more than that and the cookies will become tough.

5. Arrange the cookies at least ¾ inch apart on the baking sheets and bake for 8 minutes. Rotate the sheets top to bottom and front to back and continue to bake until they give just slightly to the touch, 4 to 6 minutes longer.

6. Let cool on the baking sheets for 5 minutes, then gently transfer to a rack (the cookies are very delicate when warm, but will become slightly sturdier as they cool). Let cool completely. Store in an airtight container.

## TO MAKE A TART CRUST

2. Turn the dough out onto a piece of plastic wrap and shape into a disk 1 inch thick. Wrap in the plastic wrap and chill in the refrigerator until firm, 1 to 2 hours or up to overnight.

3. When you're ready to bake, position a rack in the center of the oven and preheat the oven to 350°F.

4. On a lightly floured surface, roll the dough to ¼-inch thickness. Transfer to a tart pan 9 or 10 inches in diameter either by rolling the dough loosely around the rolling pin and unrolling over the pan, or by sliding the removable tart pan bottom under the dough and using it to transfer the dough into the pan. Being careful not to press or stretch the dough, gently ease the dough into the corners of the pan. Remove the excess dough along the top edge of the pan using a small knife or your fingers. Prick the bottom of the dough with a fork at 1-inch intervals.

5. Bake until the crust looks dry in the center, about 20 minutes. When you take it out of the oven, gently press down on any air bubbles that may have formed. Let cool completely on a rack.

## TO MAKE CRUMBS FOR AN ICE CREAM PIE

2. Position racks in the top and bottom thirds of the oven and preheat the oven to 350°F. Line two baking sheets with parchment paper or nonstick mats.

3. Break the dough into walnut-sized lumps with your fingers and space them evenly on the baking sheets. Bake for 10 minutes, then rotate the pans front to back and top to bottom. Continue to bake for another 10 to 15 minutes, or until they give just slightly to the touch.

4. Let cool completely on the baking sheets. Working in batches as necessary, transfer the shortbread to a food processor and pulse until it becomes a coarse meal. Store in an airtight container at room temperature.

# HOT FUDGE SAUCE

Makes about 1¼ cups | Pictured on page 197

This recipe came to us from our friend Tommy Weber. It is a rich, thick, and decadent sauce that makes any type of ice cream a real treat! The sauce has a wonderful consistency—thick and pourable when warm, it becomes ever so slightly chewy as it cools. We love the transformation that takes place as it comes in contact with ice cream.

## AT A GLANCE

SHELF LIFE: Up to 3 weeks

½ cup heavy cream

½ cup sugar

2 tablespoons Dutch-processed cocoa powder, measured then sifted

¼ cup tapioca syrup or corn syrup

½ teaspoon kosher salt

2 ounces bittersweet chocolate (about 60% cacao), finely chopped (½ cup)

2 ounces unsweetened chocolate, finely chopped (½ cup)

½ teaspoon pure vanilla extract

1.  In a medium nonreactive saucepan, stir together the cream, sugar, cocoa, tapioca syrup, and salt. Put the pan over medium-high heat, bring to a boil, and cook just until the sugar has completely dissolved. Remove from the heat.

2.  Stir in both chocolates and the vanilla until the chocolate is melted and the sauce is completely smooth. (If you have any lumps, use a spatula to gently press and smear them against the bottom of the pan as you stir.)

Serve right away or store in an airtight container in the refrigerator (it lasts for weeks, if you have that much self-restraint). To rewarm, heat in the microwave at half power for a minute or two.

**TIP:** *If some of the chocolate refuses to melt, it means the cream was not hot enough. To fix this, bring 1 inch of water to a simmer in a medium saucepan, transfer the sauce to a heatproof bowl, and put the bowl over but not touching the water. Whisk the sauce until smooth.*

**SERVE IT WITH . . .**
* Everything. Seriously. Even a spoonful in your coffee.

# CHOCOLATE GLAZE

Makes about 2 cups | Pictured on page 102

While the Hot Fudge Sauce (page 93) is thick and rich, this glaze is a little thinner in consistency and shinier in appearance. We put it between cake layers, drizzle it on pies, and dip the tops of frosted cupcakes into it. Used on ice cream cake or pies, the glaze needs to be just warm enough to pour but not hot. Work quickly to cover the surface, because it will pull away from the ice cream if you overwork it. Use 1/2 cup of glaze for an 8-inch cake.

## AT A GLANCE

SHELF LIFE: Up to 3 weeks

8 ounces bittersweet chocolate (about 60% cacao), finely chopped (3/4 cup)

3 tablespoons tapioca syrup or corn syrup

1 cup heavy cream

3 tablespoons sugar

1. Put the chocolate in a medium heatproof bowl, pour the tapioca syrup over the chocolate, and set aside.

2. Stir together the cream and sugar in a small nonreactive saucepan and put the pan over medium-high heat. When the mixture reaches a simmer (small bubbles will appear and break around the edge of the pan), remove from the heat. Stir until the sugar is dissolved. Pour the mixture over the chocolate and let stand for 1 to 2 minutes. Whisk until smooth.

Let the glaze cool slightly before using (it's too runny when it's hot). A little warmer than room temperature is ideal.

To glaze the top of an ice cream cake, pour 1/2 cup of the just-warm glaze onto the top of the cake and spread it quickly. The glaze will start to pull away from the ice cream if you overwork it, so cover the surface in a few quick spreads and place back in the freezer.

If making ahead, or if you have leftovers, transfer to a container, cover and store in the refrigerator. To rewarm, heat gently in the microwave or in a double boiler just until it's barely warm.

**TIP:** *If some of the chocolate refuses to melt, it means the cream was not hot enough. To fix this, bring 1 inch of water to a simmer in a medium saucepan, transfer the glaze to a heatproof bowl, and put the bowl over but not touching the water. Whisk the glaze until smooth.*

# CHOCOLATE BUTTERCREAM FROSTING

Makes about 3 cups (enough to frost an 8-inch cake, 16 to 18 cupcakes, or 2 ice cream cakes)

This is another old-fashioned recipe, much like the Vanilla Buttercream Frosting on page 49. Fluffy, light, and not overly sweet, it is as delicious as it is easy to make. You can use natural or Dutch-processed cocoa powder here with equally good results; the natural will give you a "milk chocolate" flavor, while the Dutch-processed will yield a darker and more intense frosting. This recipe can easily be halved.

AT A GLANCE · · · · · · · · · · · · · · · · · · · · · · · · · · · · · · · · · · · · · · · · · · · · · · · · · · · · · · · · · · · · · · · · · · · · · · · · · · · · · · · · · · · · · · · · · · · · · · · · · · · · · ·

SHELF LIFE: 2 weeks

· · · · · · · · · · · · · · · · · · · · · · · · · · · · · · · · · · · · · · · · · · · · · · · · · · · · · · · · · · · · · · · · · · · · · · · · · · · · · · · · · · · · · · · · · · · · · · · · · · · · · · · · · · · · · · · · ·

1 pound unsalted butter, at warm room temperature and cut into $1/2$-inch slices

$1^{1}/2$ cups (8 ounces) powdered sugar, measured then sifted

$2/3$ cup ($2^{1}/3$ ounces) natural or Dutch-processed cocoa powder, measured then sifted

2 tablespoons water

2 teaspoons pure vanilla extract

$1/2$ teaspoon kosher salt

1. Combine all of the ingredients in the bowl of a stand mixer with the paddle attachment. Beat first on low speed, then increase to medium-high speed and continue to beat until the frosting is light and fluffy, 3 to 4 minutes. Scrape the sides of the bowl and mix briefly again.

2. Use immediately or cover and refrigerate for up to 2 weeks. If made ahead, let the frosting come to room temperature before using and remix briefly using the stand mixer until it regains its light and fluffy consistency.

> **MAKE IT YOUR OWN**
> ❋ Add $1/4$ teaspoon peppermint extract.
> ❋ Fold in finely chopped chocolate, nuts, Almond Toffee (page 68), or Peanut Brittle (page 131).

# CHOCOLATE WHIPPED CREAM

Makes about 1¹/₂ cups

This simple recipe uses cream and bittersweet chocolate (rather than the more commonly called-for cocoa) and produces a rich and dense whipped cream, sort of like a mousse or a whipped ganache. Be sure to budget time to refrigerate the mixture, as this makes the whipping much easier.

Use this as a topping for ice cream cakes or pies, sandwiched in the middle of a layer cake, or as an accompaniment to any dessert.

## AT A GLANCE

CHILLING TIME: 1 to 2 hours          SHELF LIFE: None—use right away

3 ounces bittersweet chocolate (52% to 60% cacao), finely chopped (heaping ¹/₂ cup)

1 cup heavy cream

1. Put about 2 inches of water in the bottom of a medium saucepan and bring to a simmer over medium-high heat. Put the chocolate in a heatproof nonreactive bowl and set over but not touching the simmering water.

2. Whisk the chocolate until melted, then whisk in ¹/₄ cup of the cream. When completely smooth, add the remaining cream in ¹/₄-cup increments, blending well after each addition.

   **TIP:** *Go slowly as you add the cream; adding it too quickly will cause the chocolate to seize up.*

3. When all the cream is added and the mixture is completely smooth, remove from the heat and refrigerate for 1 to 2 hours.

4. Remove the bowl from the refrigerator and whisk by hand just until the mixture becomes fluffy. Be careful not to overwhip it, which will result in a stiff, grainy texture. (Don't be afraid to whip by hand! It takes less than a minute of whipping to achieve the right consistency, and it's very easy to overwhip this cream using a mixer.)

   Use immediately.

# CHOCOLATE SHAVINGS

Here at the Creamery we use chocolate shavings to garnish many of our desserts. We make them by scraping a large chef's knife (held both at the handle and at the tip of the knife) at an angle across the flat surface of an 11-pound block of chocolate. When the angle is perfect and the temperature of the chocolate is just right, it produces perfect curls of chocolate.

Using an 11-pound block of chocolate is obviously not practical for the home cook, but you can approximate the technique using a vegetable peeler and a large chunk of chocolate (the bigger the better). It is important to make sure your chocolate isn't too warm or too cold; close to body temperature is key to getting the desired curly shapes.

Unwrap one end of your chocolate and hold it over a clean work surface. Use your vegetable peeler to pull along one of the flat edges of the chocolate. The resulting shavings may be flaky at first, but you will get better as you practice.

Pick the curls up with an offset spatula (to minimize melting and breakage) and place them directly onto your dessert. If not using the shavings right away, transfer them to a baking sheet and hold them at room temperature (or in the refrigerator if your kitchen is particularly warm) until ready to use.

Ice cream pie made from Cookies and Cream Ice Cream (page 84), Dark Chocolate Cookie piecrust (page 90), Chocolate Whipped Cream, and Chocolate Shavings

# COFFEE and TEA

99

**IF THERE'S ONE ICE CREAM FLAVOR** that perfectly encapsulates our entire approach, it would have to be Coffee Toffee. This flavor, which also happens to be one of our most popular, embodies our commitment to using the best local ingredients and taking no shortcuts along the way. Like all of our ice creams, Coffee Toffee begins with dairy products from Straus Family Creamery in nearby Marshall, California. We make the toffee from scratch, chop it by hand, and fold it into each batch of coffee ice cream. And last but not least, we use the excellent coffee from our friends at Ritual Coffee Roasters, whose café and roasting facility is just a few blocks away from the Creamery (and whose coffee beans are pictured on page 98).

We enjoy a close relationship with the folks at Ritual, who share our commitment to operating in a sustainable manner. They source green beans direct from plantations around the world and pay a fair price that helps those growers thrive. They are also very passionate about quality and flavor and thus are always giving us new coffees to experiment with. Over the years, we've learned a lot about which types of coffee we like best, and we work closely with Ritual to find new varieties that fill the bill. It's a relationship that is both collaborative and delicious!

Coffee and tea are perfectly suited to be enjoyed as ice cream. After all, as hot beverages they're often enjoyed with cream and/or sugar, which help to smooth out the drinks' astringency and create a full and well-rounded mouthfeel. For the same reason, coffee and tea lend themselves beautifully to ice creams and granitas.

If you've ever brewed coffee or tea, you already know much of what it takes to make coffee- or tea-flavored ice cream. Both beverages are infusions: you combine coffee grounds or tea leaves with hot water, let them steep, then strain out the solids. Making ice cream with these flavors requires the same process except that we use hot cream and milk instead of water.

The ice cream recipes in this chapter include estimates for the steeping time, but your timing may vary depending on the grind of coffee or type of tea you use. Taste the mixture at several intervals throughout the steeping phase and adjust the time accordingly. Keep in mind that the final flavor will be diluted with the addition of the egg yolks and will be mellowed further upon freezing. However, be careful not to steep the tea or coffee for too long—this results in "overextraction" and allows the bitter tannins to dominate the overall flavor.

Fresh ingredients at their peak of flavor are key for brewing a full-flavored cup of coffee or tea, and it's the same when you're using them as ingredients in a recipe. If your coffee beans or tea leaves are over the hill, the end result will be muted in flavor at best and musty or off-tasting at worst.

# BUYING AND USING COFFEE

The best way to ensure you're using fresh coffee is to get it from a local roaster. These companies tend to roast frequently and in small batches, which ensures freshness.

Coffee is at its best within a couple of weeks of the roasting date, so buy only as much as you think you can use within that two-week window. Keep the coffee in a dark and airtight container at cool room temperature (not in the refrigerator or freezer, which is too humid and destroys the subtle flavors of the coffee).

> **TIP:** Look for and buy "fair trade" coffees when you can. This ensures that the coffee farmers are paid a fair price for their beans—something that is unfortunately rare within the coffee industry.

Buy whole beans and grind them yourself as you need them. Keeping the beans whole minimizes the surface area exposed to oxygen, which helps maintain the full, fresh flavor of the beans. All of the coffee recipes in this book were tested using a finely ground coffee (about one step coarser than an espresso grind). This ensures a quick steeping time, but it also means that some of the finer specks of coffee will make their way through the filter and give a bit of added texture to the final product. You can use a finer or coarser grind if you like; coarser grinds are easier to strain out but require a longer steeping time than a finer grind.

There are two main factors that influence what a coffee will taste like when it is brewed: the origin of the beans and the degree to which they are roasted. The latter doesn't just affect the coffee's intensity of flavor, it also influences the *types* of flavors it will exhibit. Lighter roasts produce caramelly and citrusy notes in the coffee, whereas darker roasts produce deeper, more chocolaty flavors.

And just as light-roast Kenyan and dark-roast Sumatran coffees taste very different from one another when brewed, those varied flavor notes really come through when they are used in ice cream or granita. At the Creamery, we use a variety of coffee blends depending on our mood and what's available, but we particularly like Ethiopian blends because of their fruity notes.

Having said that, as long as your coffee beans are fresh, you really can't go wrong. If you like to drink it, you'll probably love it in ice cream!

# BUYING AND USING TEA

Without question, you will get the best flavor by using loose whole-leaf teas. The intact leaves stay fresher longer, and they're generally of higher quality than those packaged into tea bags. Whole-leaf teas are also much easier to strain out of the steeping liquid (and, unlike coffee, little specks of tea in ice cream are not so appealing).

> **TIP:** Even if you can only find bagged tea, it still helps to cut open and empty the contents of the bags into the steeping liquid. This allows the leaves to disperse and steep more evenly.

Just about any variety of black or oolong (semi-fermented) tea can be used in these recipes. Earl Grey—black tea spiked with the essence of bergamot, a citrus fruit—is a particular favorite of ours, but feel free to use whatever strikes your fancy. However, herbal teas can often taste medicinal when used in desserts.

Store tea in an airtight container away from sunlight at cool room temperature. Kept this way, it will stay flavorful for up to a year, depending on the type.

Ice cream cake made with Coffee Toffee Ice Cream (opposite), Chocolate Midnight Cake (page 88), Chocolate Glaze (page 94), and Almond Toffee (page 68)

# COFFEE ICE CREAM

Makes about 1 quart

When we first opened the Creamery, we featured two different coffee flavors in our case: plain Coffee as well as Coffee Toffee, which was the plain coffee base with almond toffee bits folded in. The crunchy Coffee Toffee became so popular that we eventually took the plain version out of rotation. Here we offer you the original creamy base and give you the option to turn it into Coffee Toffee (see Make It Your Own, page 104).

We use finely ground coffee, which allows for some of the grounds to pass through the sieve and give some nice texture to the ice cream. For a smoother ice cream, use coarsely ground coffee beans and the finest mesh strainer you have.

The strength of flavor can also be intensified or lightened by extending or shortening your steeping time, respectively.

## AT A GLANCE

| TECHNIQUE: | SPECIAL EQUIPMENT: | INFUSING AND CHILLING TIME: | SHELF LIFE: |
|---|---|---|---|
| Ice cream (page 12) | Ice cream machine | 2 hours or overnight | 1 week |

1³/₄ cups heavy cream

³/₄ cup 1% or 2% milk

¹/₂ cup sugar

¹/₄ cup (³/₄ ounce) finely ground coffee

¹/₄ teaspoon kosher salt

5 large egg yolks

### INFUSE THE MILK/CREAM

1. In a nonreactive heavy saucepan, stir together the cream, milk, half of the sugar (¹/₄ cup), coffee, and salt.

2. Put the pan over medium-high heat. When the mixture just begins to bubble around the edges, remove from the heat and cover the pan. Let steep for about 10 minutes, or until the cream has taken on a strong coffee flavor. (Stir occasionally and taste it to monitor the progress.)

### MAKE THE BASE

3. In a medium heatproof bowl, whisk the yolks just to break them up, then whisk in the remaining half of the sugar (¹/₄ cup). Uncover the cream mixture and put the pan over medium heat.

4. Carefully scoop out about ¹/₂ cup of the hot cream mixture and, whisking the eggs constantly, add the cream to the bowl with the egg yolks. Repeat, adding another ¹/₂ cup of the hot cream to the bowl with the yolks. Using a heatproof rubber spatula, stir the cream in the saucepan as you slowly pour the egg-and-cream mixture from the bowl into the pan.

5. Cook the mixture carefully over medium heat, stirring constantly, until it is thickened, coats the back of a spatula, and holds a clear

CONTINUED

path when you run your finger across the spatula, 3 minutes longer.

6. Strain the base through a fine-mesh strainer into a clean container. Set the container into an ice-water bath, wash your spatula, and use it to stir the base occasionally until it is cool. Remove the container from the ice-water bath, cover with plastic wrap, and refrigerate the base for at least 2 hours or overnight.

### FREEZE THE ICE CREAM

7. Freeze in your ice cream machine according to the manufacturer's instructions. While the ice cream is churning, put the container you'll use to store the ice cream into the freezer. Enjoy right away or, for a firmer ice cream, transfer to the chilled container and freeze for at least 4 hours.

---

**MAKE IT YOUR OWN**

* Add 1 cup finely chopped Almond Toffee (page 68) in the last minute of churning to make Coffee Toffee. It's one of our "greatest hits" and super good!
* Swirl in 1/3 to 1/2 cup of Fudge Ripple (page 122) for a mocha effect.

**SERVE IT WITH . . .**

* Ricanelas Ice Cream (page 188) to emulate a cinnamon cappuccino
* Vanilla Ice Cream (page 35)—the Coffee Ice Cream makes the vanilla seem even creamier!
* A sprinkle of Almond Toffee (page 68) and a drizzle of Hot Fudge Sauce (page 93)

---

# ESPRESSO FUDGE SAUCE

Makes about 1 cup

This versatile sauce has a nice shine and wonderful deep chocolate flavor. If you do not want the coffee flavor you can replace the espresso with water.

AT A GLANCE ···············································································································

SHELF LIFE: up to 3 weeks
·····································································································································

$1/2$ cup sugar

$1/4$ cup water

$1 3/4$ ounces ($1/2$ cup) Dutch-processed cocoa powder, measured then sifted

1 ounce bittersweet chocolate, finely chopped (scant $1/4$ cup)

$1/4$ teaspoon kosher salt

$1/2$ cup freshly brewed espresso or very strong coffee

$1/2$ teaspoon pure vanilla extract

1. Mix the sugar and water in a small saucepan. Dip your fingers or a pastry brush in water and wash down the sides of the pan (stray sugar crystals can prevent the syrup from melting evenly). Put the pan over medium-high heat, bring to a boil, and cook until the sugar is completely dissolved. Remove from the heat.

2. Combine the cocoa powder, chopped chocolate, and salt in a medium heatproof bowl.

3. Pour the sugar syrup over the chocolate and let stand without stirring for 1 to 2 minutes. Whisk until smooth and slowly whisk in the espresso and vanilla.

   Let the sauce cool slightly and use warm or at room temperature.

   Transfer any unused sauce to a covered container and store in the refrigerator. Rewarm before using.

# ESPRESSO GRANITA

Makes about 1½ quarts

This adults-only granita pairs well with a dollop of lightly whipped cream and a few cookies or with a scoop of vanilla ice cream (or any other flavor that you like with coffee).

The recipe calls for 3½ cups of very strong coffee. You can pull a lot of shots of espresso, or you can use a very fine grind of dark roast coffee and brew it in a French press, which will give you coffee that is full-bodied and flavorful enough to approximate espresso.

## AT A GLANCE

| TECHNIQUE: | SPECIAL EQUIPMENT: | FREEZING TIME: | SHELF LIFE: |
|---|---|---|---|
| Granita (page 18) | Espresso maker or French coffee press | 4 hours | 1 week |

3½ cups freshly brewed espresso or very strong coffee

¾ cup sugar

### MAKE THE BASE

1. Combine the espresso and sugar in a medium bowl and stir until all the sugar has dissolved.

### FREEZE THE GRANITA

2. Pour into a 9 by 13-inch baking dish or similar shallow pan. Freeze uncovered for 1½ hours, or until ice crystals start to form.

3. Stir the mixture with a fork to break up the crystals. Return the baking dish to the freezer and stir every 30 minutes or so to break up the ice crystals as the granita freezes. When the granita is completely frozen (about 4 hours total), it should have a light, feathery texture.

Serve right away or transfer the granita to a container and store in the freezer. Break up the mixture with a fork just before serving.

### SERVE IT WITH . . .

❊ Brown Butter Pecan Ice Cream (page 124)

❊ A dollop of whipped cream—either vanilla (page 51) or chocolate (page 96)—for a cappuccino effect

Espresso Granita with Whipped Cream (page 51)

# GREEN TEA ICE CREAM

Makes about 1 quart

When making green tea ice cream, it is best to use finely ground green tea powder, called *matcha*, which easily dissolves into the milk and cream and infuses the ice cream base with a full flavor. You can find it in the tea section of some supermarkets or buy it from a tea specialist (see Sources on page 210).

AT A GLANCE ..........................................................................................

| TECHNIQUE: | SPECIAL EQUIPMENT: | CHILLING TIME: | SHELF LIFE: |
|---|---|---|---|
| Ice cream (page 12) | Ice cream machine | 2 hours or overnight | 1 week |

5 large egg yolks
1 tablespoon *matcha* powder
3/4 cup sugar
1 3/4 cups heavy cream
3/4 cup 1% or 2% milk
1/4 teaspoon kosher salt

## MAKE THE BASE

1. In a medium heatproof bowl, whisk the yolks just to break them up, then whisk in the *matcha* and half of the sugar (6 tablespoons). Try to make sure that the *matcha* is evenly distributed and not clumpy. Set aside.

2. In a heavy nonreactive saucepan, stir together the cream, milk, salt, and the remaining sugar (6 tablespoons) and put the pan over medium-high heat. When the mixture approaches a bare simmer, reduce the heat to medium.

3. Carefully scoop out about 1/2 cup of the hot cream mixture and, whisking the eggs constantly, add the cream to the bowl with the egg yolks. Repeat, adding another 1/2 cup of the hot cream to the bowl with the yolks. Using a heatproof rubber spatula, stir the cream in the saucepan as you slowly pour the egg-and-cream mixture from the bowl into the pan.

4. Cook the mixture carefully over medium heat, stirring constantly, until it is thickened, coats the back of a spatula, and holds a clear path when you run your finger across the spatula, about 1 to 2 minutes longer

5. Strain the base through a fine-mesh strainer into a clean container. (Don't worry if you still have a few tiny clumps of *matcha* powder; they'll smooth out as the ice cream churns.) Set the container into an ice-water bath, wash your spatula, and use it to stir the base occasionally until it is cool. Remove the container from the ice-water bath, cover with plastic wrap, and refrigerate the base for at least 2 hours or overnight.

## FREEZE THE ICE CREAM

6. Freeze in your ice cream machine according to the manufacturer's instructions. While the ice cream is churning, put the container you'll use to store the ice cream into the freezer. Enjoy right away or, for a firmer ice cream, transfer to the chilled container and freeze for at least 4 hours.

# EARL GREY ICE CREAM

Makes about 1 quart

We tried many types of tea before settling on this one for our ice cream. Earl Grey, a black tea infused with the citrus fruit bergamot, has a distinctive fruity flavor that really comes through even when combined with milk, cream, sugar, and eggs and frozen into ice cream. Other black teas will work well in this recipe, too. Whichever kind of tea it is, be sure that it is good, fresh loose-leaf tea. Older tea will not have as much flavor and will require a longer steeping time.

To prevent little bits of tea leaves from infiltrating the final product, use the finest-mesh strainer you have.

## AT A GLANCE

| TECHNIQUE: | SPECIAL EQUIPMENT: | INFUSING AND CHILLING TIME: | SHELF LIFE: |
|---|---|---|---|
| Ice cream (page 12) | Ice cream machine | 2 hours or overnight | 1 week |

1³/₄ cups heavy cream

³/₄ cup 1% or 2% milk

¹/₂ cup sugar

3 tablespoons loose-leaf Earl Grey tea

¹/₄ teaspoon kosher salt

5 large egg yolks

### INFUSE THE MILK/CREAM

1. In a heavy nonreactive saucepan, stir together the cream, milk, half of the sugar (¹/₄ cup), the tea, and salt.

2. Put the pan over medium-high heat. When the mixture just begins to bubble around the edges, remove from the heat and cover the pan. Let steep for about 10 minutes, or until the cream has taken on the distinct flavor of Earl Grey tea. (Stir occasionally and taste it to monitor the progress.)

### MAKE THE BASE

3. In a medium heatproof bowl, whisk the yolks just to break them up, then whisk in the remaining half of the sugar (¹/₄ cup). Uncover the cream mixture and put the pan over medium heat.

4. Carefully scoop out about ¹/₂ cup of the hot cream mixture and, whisking the eggs constantly, add the cream to the bowl with the egg yolks. Repeat, adding another ¹/₂ cup of the hot cream to the bowl with the yolks. Using a heatproof rubber spatula, stir the cream in the saucepan as you slowly pour the egg-and-cream mixture from the bowl into the pan.

5. Cook the mixture carefully over medium heat, stirring constantly, until it is thickened, coats the back of a spatula, and holds a clear path when you run your finger across the spatula, about 3 minutes longer.

6. Strain the base through a fine-mesh strainer into a clean container. Set the container

CONTINUED

into an ice-water bath, wash your spatula, and use it to stir the base occasionally until it is cool. Remove the container from the ice-water bath, cover with plastic wrap, and refrigerate the base for at least 2 hours or overnight.

### FREEZE THE ICE CREAM

7. Freeze in your ice cream machine according to the manufacturer's instructions. While the ice cream is churning, put the container you'll use to store the ice cream into the freezer. Enjoy right away or, for a firmer ice cream, transfer to the chilled container and freeze for at least 4 hours.

**MAKE IT YOUR OWN**

❊ Use any high-quality loose-leaf tea. Oolong is especially good.

**SERVE IT WITH . . .**

❊ Orange-Cardamom Ice Cream (page 158)
❊ Hot Fudge Sauce (page 93) or Caramel Sauce (page 71)
❊ Shortbread (page 44) or Chocolate Shortbread (page 91)

# EARL GREY SPRITZ COOKIES

Makes about 3 dozen cookies

Spritz cookies, made by extruding soft cookie dough through a special press fitted with a decorative die, have an undeniable nostalgia factor for us. They are pretty and festive, and we always make a few flavors of them during the holidays.

These unique and aromatic cookies get their flavor by infusing the butter with Earl Grey tea. It is a very easy recipe, but be sure to set aside enough time to chill everything. Plan on 3 hours to chill the butter and another 2 hours for the dough. You can infuse and chill the butter a day or two in advance of making the dough.

Most people don't have a cookie press, so the recipe below describes shaping the dough into balls by hand. If you have a press, however, you should use it. Just skip the step where you chill the dough, which would make it too stiff to go through the die.

### AT A GLANCE

CHILLING TIME: 3 hours for the butter, plus 2 hours or up to overnight for the dough

SHELF LIFE: 5 days

1 cup (8 ounces) unsalted butter, cut into 1-inch cubes

3 tablespoons loose-leaf Earl Grey tea

1 tablespoon bergamot olive oil (see Note)

2¼ cups (10 ounces) unbleached all-purpose flour

1 teaspoon kosher salt

¾ cup (3½ ounces) powdered sugar, measured then sifted, plus about ½ cup more for rolling

2 large egg yolks

1 teaspoon pure vanilla extract

1. Combine the butter, tea leaves, and olive oil in a small saucepan and put the pan over medium heat. Stir frequently until the butter is completely melted. Remove from the heat, cover, and let steep for 15 minutes. Strain the butter through a fine-mesh strainer and into a heatproof bowl. Refrigerate until solid, about 3 hours.

2. In a medium bowl, whisk together the flour and salt and set aside.

3. Remove the chilled butter from the refrigerator and transfer it to the bowl of a stand mixer with the paddle attachment, breaking it into 1- to 2-inch chunks as you go. Add the ¾ cup powdered sugar.

   Mix on low speed at first, and then increase to medium speed and continue mixing until the mixture is smooth, 1½ to 2 minutes. Scrape down the bowl and, with the motor running, add the egg yolks one at a time, completely mixing in each yolk before adding the next. Add the vanilla and mix to blend. Scrape down the sides of the bowl, add the flour mixture, and mix on low speed just until the dough comes together, about 30 seconds.

4. Cover the bowl with plastic wrap and chill until the dough is firm, at least 2 hours or up to overnight.

5. When you're ready to bake, position racks in the top and bottom thirds of the oven and preheat the oven to 350°F. Line two baking sheets with parchment paper or non-stick mats. Scoop up 1 tablespoon of dough and form the dough into a ball. Repeat until all the dough has been shaped. Place the balls 2 inches apart on the baking sheets. Flatten the balls slightly with the palm of your hand so that they're about ½ inch thick.

6. Bake for 7 minutes, then rotate the baking sheets top to bottom and front to back. Continue to bake until the cookies are golden brown on the edges, 8 to 9 minutes longer.

   Let the cookies cool for a minute on the baking sheet, then transfer to a cooling rack. Once the cookies are completely cool, roll in the ½ cup powdered sugar. Store in an airtight container.

**NOTE:** The bergamot olive oil we use is made by pressing bergamots (the citrus fruit that gives Earl Grey tea its unique flavor) with ripe olives to produce an aromatic, citrusy olive oil. If you can't find bergamot olive oil, you can substitute blood orange or lemon olive oil (which are made in the same way) or extra-virgin olive oil.

**SERVE IT WITH . . .**
❊ Chocolate Ice Cream (page 78)

# NUTS

NUTS ARE BY FAR our most popular ice cream topping. They're classic, of course, beloved for their toasty flavor and the textural contrast they add to a creamy scoop. We offer quite an array to meet the demand: macadamia nuts, spiced pecans, walnuts, toasted almonds, salted peanuts, pistachios, and Marcona almonds! Those last ones, Marcona almonds, are a Spanish variety typically served blanched, toasted, and salted. They are a favorite of many guests, who savor them for their crunchy, salty, buttery, fatty deliciousness. Other guests might not be familiar with them, but whenever we offer them a taste, they immediately respond with, "*Yeah,* I'll have that!" We love converting folks to that special Spanish treat.

## BUYING AND USING NUTS

If you can, buy your nuts from bulk bins, typically found at natural foods stores. There are two significant benefits to this: first, you'll pay less per pound compared to prepackaged nuts, and, second, you can smell and taste the nuts before buying them.

But what are you smelling and tasting for? Freshness, mainly. Nuts have a high fat content, which makes them prone to turning rancid. Fresh nuts will smell and taste like, well, what you'd expect. Rancid nuts have a heavy, "off" smell that is reminiscent of petroleum or pencil erasers and will ruin your dish. Steer clear of those!

Most of our recipes call for chopped nuts, but we recommend buying whole nuts and chopping them yourself as you need them. The convenience offered by prechopped nuts is pretty minor, and they have a shorter shelf life due to their greater surface area. Whole nuts will last longer and give you the freedom to chop or grind them however the recipe specifies.

Your freezer is the best place to store nuts. Kept in a sealed freezer bag with any excess air squeezed out, nuts will stay fresh for at least a year. (Most cabinets are too warm and will encourage the nuts to go rancid.)

We also recommend buying raw nuts and toasting them yourself before using them. Toasting helps to enhance and develop the nuts' flavor, and doing it yourself (rather than buying preroasted nuts) gives you more control over the degree to which the nuts are toasted and browned. You can toast nuts up to two weeks before using them. If you can only find roasted nuts at the grocery store, they'll still benefit from a brief toasting to reawaken their flavor. Just watch extra carefully that they don't burn.

The best way to toast nuts is to spread them in a single layer on a rimmed baking sheet and bake in a preheated 350°F oven until golden and aromatic. Whole nuts take longer to toast than chopped ones do (about 15 minutes versus 5 to 10 minutes), but whole nuts toast more evenly; with chopped nuts, the tiny pieces turn dark brown well before the larger ones do. Let

coarse          medium          fine

the nuts cool completely before chopping them or adding them to a recipe so they have time to get crunchy again; they are too soft and rubbery when they're warm.

> **TIP:** *In a pinch, you can use the broiler to toast nuts. The results are not as even, though, and you have to toss the nuts frequently to prevent burning. Still, it's a lot faster and a little more energy efficient if you have no other need to heat the entire oven.*

A chef's knife is the best tool for chopping nuts; if you use a blender or food processor, the pieces will be much less even in size and you risk overprocessing. (If you do use a blender or food processor, be sure to pulse them as opposed to simply ginding them to keep them from turning into nut butter.) After every few chops, regather the nuts into a pile. The smaller nuts will sink to the bottom and the larger pieces will surface at the top. Gently sweep the top pieces off to the side to continue chopping, and leave the smaller pieces as they are.

Here's a rundown of the terms we use to describe the size of chopped nuts:

- Coarsely chopped = pieces ⅓ to ½ inch
- Chopped = pieces ¼ inch
- Finely chopped = pieces ⅛ inch

We do use a food processor when we want pulverized or ground nuts, such as for the Pistachio Ice Cream on page 119. In this case, the extra surface area of the ground nuts provides a more rapid and thorough infusion of the flavor into the base. Just be careful to pulse the food processor (rather than run the machine continuously) to keep the nuts cool, as overheating will cause the nuts' oils to separate out. These ground nuts are then combined with the hot cream and milk mixture and allowed to infuse. A very fine mesh strainer (sometimes called a *chinois*) is the ideal tool for straining the mixture afterward, as its close-laid wires catch even the tiniest ground-nut particles and will produce a perfectly smooth and creamy ice cream. A regular fine-mesh strainer will also work, but it will produce a more rustic-textured ice cream.

> **TIP:** *Nuts all have different flavors, but you can usually exchange one for another in recipes. Just make sure the flavors play well together. Walnuts, for instance, are much more assertive than almonds and will boast a bolder flavor in your final product.*

Top: Pink Grapefruit Sorbet (page 161); bottom: Cherry Almond Ice Cream

# CHERRY ALMOND ICE CREAM

Makes about 1 quart

When we worked at the restaurant 42 Degrees, the co-owner (and our friend) Katie Dyer would eagerly anticipate the arrival of summer's cherries, because it meant we would soon be making her favorite flavor of ice cream. It takes a little time to pit the cherries, but you'll find the effort well worth the sublime taste combination of toasted almonds and sweet cherries. Make this as soon as you see cherries looking wonderful at the market because they don't stay around for long!

The type of strainer you use will have a significant impact on the texture of this ice cream. A superfine-mesh strainer (called a *chinois*) will produce a very smooth ice cream, while a regular fine-mesh wire strainer will produce a more rustic-textured ice cream.

## AT A GLANCE

| TECHNIQUE: | SPECIAL EQUIPMENT: | INFUSING AND CHILLING TIME: | SHELF LIFE: |
|---|---|---|---|
| Ice cream (page 12) | Ice cream machine | 20 minutes, plus 2 hours or overnight | 1 week |

**FOR THE CHERRIES**

2¼ cups sugar

1½ cups water

2 cups cherries

**FOR THE BASE**

¾ cup whole raw almonds

¾ cup sugar

2 cups heavy cream

1 cup 1% or 2% milk

¼ teaspoon kosher salt

5 large egg yolks

### POACH THE CHERRIES

1. In a small nonreactive saucepan, combine the 2¼ cups sugar and the water and bring to a boil over medium-high heat. When it reaches a boil, reduce the heat to maintain a gentle simmer, add the cherries, and cook until the cherries are soft and cooked through, about 5 minutes.

2. Remove from the heat and let the cherries cool completely in the syrup. (You can do this step a day ahead; transfer the cherries in the syrup to a covered container and refrigerate until ready to churn the ice cream.)

3. Once cool, drain the cherries (save the syrup for other uses) and squeeze the pits out of the fruit. Chop the cherries into ¼-inch pieces. Refrigerate until you're ready to churn the ice cream.

   **TIP:** *The leftover syrup is infused with lots of fabulous cherry flavor. Drizzle it over ice cream, swirl it into club soda, or use it in our recipes calling for simple syrup.*

### PREPARE THE NUTS

4. Position a rack in the center of the oven and preheat the oven to 350°F.

5. Spread the almonds on a rimmed baking sheet. Bake until the nuts are golden brown

CONTINUED

and smell nutty, about 15 minutes. Let cool completely.

6. Combine the cooled nuts and the ¾ cup sugar in a food processor. Pulse until very finely ground (about the consistency of sand). Do not overprocess or the mixture will become oily and pasty.

## INFUSE THE MILK/CREAM

7. Transfer the almond mixture to a heavy nonreactive saucepan and stir in the cream, milk, and salt.

8. Uncover the cream mixture and put the pan over medium-high heat. When the mixture just begins to bubble around the edges, remove from the heat and cover the pan. Let steep for about 20 minutes, or until a distinct almond flavor has infused into the mixture. (Taste it to monitor the progress.)

## MAKE THE BASE

9. In a medium heatproof bowl, whisk the yolks just to break them up. Set aside.

10. Put the pan over medium-high heat. When the mixture approaches a bare simmer, reduce the heat to medium.

11. Carefully scoop out about ½ cup of the hot cream mixture and, whisking the eggs constantly, add the cream to the bowl with the egg yolks. Repeat, adding another ½ cup of the hot cream to the bowl with the yolks. Using a heatproof rubber spatula, stir the cream in the saucepan as you slowly pour the egg-and-cream mixture from the bowl into the pan.

12. Cook the mixture carefully over medium heat, stirring constantly, until it is thickened, coats the back of a spatula, and holds a clear

path when you run your finger across the spatula, 1 to 2 minutes longer.

13. Strain the base through a fine-mesh strainer into a clean container. Set the container into an ice-water bath, wash your spatula, and use it to stir the base occasionally until it is cool. Remove the container from the ice-water bath, cover with plastic wrap, and refrigerate the base for at least 2 hours or overnight.

## FREEZE THE ICE CREAM

14. Freeze in your ice cream machine according to the manufacturer's instructions. While the ice cream is churning, put the container you'll use to store the ice cream into the freezer. Add the chopped cherries in the last minute or so of churning, or fold them in by hand after transferring the ice cream to the chilled container.

Enjoy right away or, for a firmer ice cream, freeze for at least 4 hours.

> **SERVE IT WITH . . .**
> ❋ Hot Fudge Sauce (page 93)
> ❋ Chocolate Shortbread piecrust (page 91) and Whipped Cream (page 51) to make an ice cream pie

# PISTACHIO ICE CREAM

Makes about 1 quart

To make ice cream, we prefer to start with raw pistachios and toast them very lightly in the oven. We want to enhance and intensify their flavor without losing the delicate, almost fruity quality of the raw nuts. It can be difficult to find raw pistachios, especially ones that are already shelled. If you can't get any, buy the toasted kind and skip the toasting step.

As for the Cherry Almond Ice cream (page 117), the type of strainer you use will have a significant impact on the texture of the ice cream. A *chinois* will yield a very smooth ice cream, while a regular fine-mesh strainer will give you a more rustic result.

## AT A GLANCE

| TECHNIQUE: | SPECIAL EQUIPMENT: | INFUSING AND CHILLING TIME: | SHELF LIFE: |
| --- | --- | --- | --- |
| Ice cream (page 12) | Ice cream machine | 2 hours or overnight | 1 week |

3/4 cup raw shelled pistachios

3/4 cup sugar

2 cups heavy cream

1 1/4 cups 1% or 2% milk

1/4 teaspoon kosher salt

5 large egg yolks

### PREPARE THE NUTS

1. Position a rack in the center of the oven and preheat the oven to 350°F.

2. Spread the pistachios on a rimmed baking sheet. Bake until the nuts are just starting to brown and smell nutty, 5 to 6 minutes. Let cool completely.

3. Combine the cooled nuts and the sugar in the bowl of a food processor. Pulse until very finely ground (about the consistency of sand). Do not overprocess or the mixture will become oily and pasty.

### INFUSE THE MILK/CREAM

4. Transfer the pistachio mixture to a heavy nonreactive saucepan and stir in the cream, milk, and salt.

5. Put the pan over medium-high heat. When the mixture just begins to bubble around the edges, remove from the heat and cover the pan. Let steep for 15 to 20 minutes, or until a distinct pistachio flavor has infused into the mixture. (Taste it to monitor the progress.)

### MAKE THE BASE

6. In a medium heatproof bowl, whisk the yolks just to break them up. Set aside.

7. Uncover the cream mixture and put the pan over medium-high heat. When the mixture approaches a bare simmer, reduce the heat to medium.

8. Carefully scoop out about 1/2 cup of the hot cream mixture and, whisking the eggs constantly, add the cream to the bowl with the egg yolks. Repeat, adding another 1/2 cup of

CONTINUED

the hot cream to the bowl with the yolks. Using a heatproof rubber spatula, stir the cream in the saucepan as you slowly pour the egg-and-cream mixture from the bowl into the pan.

9. Cook the mixture carefully over medium heat, stirring constantly, until it is thickened, coats the back of a spatula, and holds a clear path when you run your finger across the spatula, 1 to 2 minutes longer.

10. Strain the base through a fine-mesh strainer into a clean container. Set the container into an ice-water bath, wash your spatula, and use it to stir the base occasionally until it is cool. Remove the container from the ice-water bath, cover with plastic wrap, and refrigerate the base for at least 2 hours or overnight.

## FREEZE THE ICE CREAM

11. Freeze in your ice cream machine according to the manufacturer's instructions. While the ice cream is churning, put the container you'll use to store the ice cream into the freezer. Enjoy right away or, for a firmer ice cream, transfer to the chilled container and freeze for at least 4 hours.

### MAKE IT YOUR OWN

❋ Use almonds, hazelnuts, peanuts, pecans, walnuts, or cashews in place of the pistachios.

### SERVE IT WITH . . .

❋ Balsamic Strawberry Ice Cream (page 138)
❋ Vanilla Ice Cream (page 35)
❋ Crème Fraîche Ice Cream (page 38) and Hot Fudge Sauce (page 93) to make a sundae

# ALMOND FUDGE RIPPLE ICE CREAM

Makes about 1 quart

To help our almond ice cream stand up to the more assertive flavor of the fudge swirl, we give it a boost with almond extract in this recipe. Be sure to use pure almond extract rather than the artificial stuff.

## AT A GLANCE

| TECHNIQUE: | SPECIAL EQUIPMENT: | CHILLING TIME: | SHELF LIFE: |
|---|---|---|---|
| Ice cream (page 12) | Ice cream machine | 2 hours or overnight | 1 week |

5 large egg yolks

1/2 cup sugar

2 cups heavy cream

1 cup 1% or 2% milk

1/4 teaspoon kosher salt

1/4 teaspoon almond extract

1/2 cup chopped toasted almonds (see page 114)

1/3 to 1/2 cup Fudge Ripple (page 122)

### MAKE THE BASE

1. In a medium heatproof bowl, whisk the yolks just to break them up, then whisk in half of the sugar (1/4 cup). Set aside.

2. In a heavy nonreactive saucepan, stir together the cream, milk, salt, and the remaining sugar (1/4 cup) and put the pan over medium-high heat. When the mixture approaches a bare simmer, reduce the heat to medium.

3. Carefully scoop out about 1/2 cup of the hot cream mixture and, whisking the eggs constantly, add the cream to the bowl with the egg yolks. Repeat, adding another 1/2 cup of the hot cream to the bowl with the yolks. Using a heatproof rubber spatula, stir the cream in the saucepan as you slowly pour the egg-and-cream mixture from the bowl into the pan.

4. Cook the mixture carefully over medium heat, stirring constantly, until it is thickened, coats the back of a spatula, and holds a clear path when you run your finger across the spatula, 1 to 2 minutes longer.

5. Strain the base through a fine-mesh strainer into a clean container. Set the container into an ice-water bath, wash your spatula, and use it to stir the base occasionally until it is cool. Remove the container from the ice-water bath, cover with plastic wrap, and refrigerate the base for at least 2 hours or overnight.

### FREEZE THE ICE CREAM

6. Whisk the almond extract into the chilled base.

7. Freeze in your ice cream machine according to the manufacturer's instructions. While the ice cream is churning, put the container you'll use to store the ice cream into the freezer. Add the almonds in the last minute or so of churning, or fold them in by hand after the ice cream comes out of the machine.

8. As you transfer the ice cream to the storage container, drizzle in some of the Fudge Ripple after every few spoonfuls of ice cream.

CONTINUED

When all the ice cream is in the container, use a chopstick or butter knife to gently swirl the mixture. Enjoy right away or, for a firmer ice cream, freeze for at least 4 hours.

> **MAKE IT YOUR OWN**
> ✳ Use pistachios in place of almonds.
>
> **SERVE IT WITH . . .**
> ✳ Peach Leaf Ice Cream (page 184), Ricanelas Ice Cream (page 188), or Toasted Coconut Ice Cream (page 200)
> ✳ Raspberry Swirl Sauce (page 142)

# FUDGE RIPPLE

Makes about 1 1/3 cups

We use this ripple in our Almond Fudge Ripple (page 121) as well as our Peanut Butter Fudge Swirl (opposite). You can use it anytime you want to add a ribbon of fudge to your ice cream. Leftovers can be used to make chocolate milkshakes or as a topping for ice cream.

**AT A GLANCE** · · · · · · · · · · · · · · · · · · · · · · · · · · · · · · · · · · · · · · · · · · · · · · · · · · · · · · · · · · · · · · · · · · · · · · · · · · · · · · ·

SHELF LIFE: up to 4 weeks

· · · · · · · · · · · · · · · · · · · · · · · · · · · · · · · · · · · · · · · · · · · · · · · · · · · · · · · · · · · · · · · · · · · · · · · · · · · · · · ·

1/2 cup plus 2 tablespoons sugar

1/2 cup water

6 tablespoons Dutch-processed cocoa, measured then sifted

1/4 cup tapioca syrup or corn syrup

1/8 teaspoon kosher salt

1 ounce bittersweet chocolate (about 60% cacao), finely chopped (1/4 cup)

1/2 teaspoon pure vanilla extract

1. In a small saucepan, whisk together the sugar, water, cocoa, tapioca syrup, and salt and put the pan over medium-high heat. Whisk frequently as the mixture comes to a simmer.

2. When the sugar has completely dissolved, remove from the heat. Add the chocolate and let sit undisturbed for a minute to allow the heat of the syrup to melt the chocolate.

3. Whisk until smooth, then whisk in the vanilla extract.

4. Transfer to an airtight container and refrigerate until completely chilled. Use the ripple cold (otherwise it will melt your just-churned ice cream when it's swirled in).

# PEANUT BUTTER FUDGE SWIRL ICE CREAM

Makes about 1 quart

For those who love peanut butter cups, this is the perfect flavor for you! We prefer to use natural peanut butter, which isn't as cloyingly sweet as the more processed varieties. This ice cream firms up quite a bit in the freezer; give it a few minutes at room temperature to soften before scooping.

AT A GLANCE ························································································

| TECHNIQUE: | SPECIAL EQUIPMENT: | CHILLING TIME: | SHELF LIFE: |
|---|---|---|---|
| Ice cream (page 12) | Ice cream machine | 2 hours or overnight | 1 week |

5 large egg yolks

$3/4$ cup sugar

$1/3$ cup smooth natural peanut butter

$13/4$ cups heavy cream

$3/4$ cup 1% or 2% milk

$1/2$ teaspoon kosher salt

$1/3$ cup Fudge Ripple (opposite)

## MAKE THE BASE

1. In a medium heatproof bowl, whisk the yolks just to break them up, then whisk in half of the sugar (6 tablespoons). Put the peanut butter in another heatproof bowl and set both bowls aside.

2. In a heavy nonreactive saucepan, stir together the cream, milk, salt, and the remaining sugar and put the pan over medium-high heat. When the mixture approaches a bare simmer, reduce the heat to medium.

3. Carefully scoop out about $1/2$ cup of the hot cream mixture and, whisking the eggs constantly, add the cream to the bowl with the egg yolks. Repeat, adding another $1/2$ cup of the hot cream to the bowl with the yolks. Using a heatproof rubber spatula, stir the cream in the saucepan as you slowly pour the egg-and-cream mixture from the bowl into the pan.

4. Cook the mixture carefully over medium heat, stirring constantly, until it is thickened, coats the back of a spatula, and holds a clear path when you run your finger across the spatula, 1 to 2 minutes longer.

5. Strain the base through a fine-mesh strainer into the bowl with the peanut butter and stir to combine. Set the container into an ice-water bath, wash your spatula, and use it to stir the base occasionally until it is cool. Remove the container from the ice-water bath, cover with plastic wrap, and refrigerate the base for at least 2 hours or overnight.

## FREEZE THE ICE CREAM

6. Freeze in your ice cream machine according to the manufacturer's instructions. While the ice cream is churning, put the container you'll use to store the ice cream into the freezer.

7. As you transfer the ice cream to the storage container, drizzle in some of the Fudge Ripple after every few spoonfuls of ice cream. When all the ice cream is in the container, use a chopstick or butter knife to gently swirl the mixture. Enjoy right away or, for a firmer ice cream, freeze for at least 4 hours.

# BROWN BUTTER PECAN ICE CREAM

Makes about 1 quart

Most commercially made butter pecan ice cream contains artificial butter flavor—yuck! Our recipe, inspired by local pastry chef Emily Luchetti, uses the real thing and goes a step further by using browned butter, which is a perfect complement to toasty pecans. Butter is browned by cooking it carefully over low heat until the milk solids darken and develop a nutty flavor. We take it to a deep hazelnut color to ensure the flavor comes through even after the butter is combined with the base.

## AT A GLANCE

| TECHNIQUE: | SPECIAL EQUIPMENT: | CHILLING TIME: | SHELF LIFE: |
|---|---|---|---|
| Ice cream (page 12) | Ice cream machine | 2 hours or overnight | 1 week |

5 large egg yolks

3/4 cup sugar

13/4 cups heavy cream

1/4 cup (2 ounces) unsalted butter

3/4 cup 1% or 2% milk

1/4 teaspoon kosher salt

1 teaspoon pure vanilla extract

3/4 cup chopped toasted pecans (see page 114)

### MAKE THE BASE

1. In a medium heatproof bowl, whisk the yolks just to break them up, then whisk in half of the sugar (6 tablespoons). Set aside. Set the cream by the stove.

2. Put the butter in a heavy nonreactive saucepan and put the pan over medium heat. The butter will melt and bubble, and after a few minutes it will start to turn brown. Continue to cook until it has a rich, nutty smell and the butter solids (the little specks floating around in the liquid) have turned a dark brown, 6 to 8 minutes total.

Add the cream to the pan and stir until blended. (It's important to mix in the cream before adding the milk to prevent the mixture from breaking.) Add the milk, salt, and the remaining sugar (6 tablespoons) and increase the heat to medium-high. When the mixture approaches a bare simmer, reduce the heat to medium.

3. Carefully scoop out about 1/2 cup of the hot cream mixture and, whisking the eggs constantly, add the cream to the bowl with the egg yolks. Repeat, adding another 1/2 cup of the hot cream to the bowl with the yolks. Using a heatproof rubber spatula, stir the cream in the saucepan as you slowly pour the egg-and-cream mixture from the bowl into the pan.

4. Cook the mixture carefully over medium heat, stirring constantly, until it is thickened, coats the back of a spatula, and holds a clear path when you run your finger across the spatula, 1 to 2 minutes longer.

5. Strain the base through a fine-mesh strainer into a clean container. Set the container into an ice-water bath, wash your spatula, and use it to stir the base occasionally until it is cool. Remove the container from the ice-water bath, cover with plastic wrap, and refrigerate the base for at least 2 hours or overnight.

### FREEZE THE ICE CREAM

6. Add the vanilla to the chilled base and stir until blended.

7. Freeze in your ice cream machine according to the manufacturer's instructions. While the ice cream is churning, put the container you'll use to store the ice cream into the freezer. Add the pecans in the last minute or so of churning, or fold them in by hand after transferring the ice cream to the chilled container. Enjoy right away or, for a firmer ice cream, freeze for at least 4 hours.

**SERVE IT WITH . . .**

❋ Chocolate Ice Cream (page 78), Caramelized Banana Ice Cream (page 202), or Salted Caramel Ice Cream (page 61)

❋ Great Yellow Cake (page 42), Caramel Sauce (page 71), and Spiced Pecans (page 132) for an autumnal ice cream cake

# MALTED VANILLA ICE CREAM *with*
# PEANUT BRITTLE *and* MILK CHOCOLATE PIECES

Makes about 1 quart

Like the Malted Milk Chocolate Ice Cream on page 82, this recipe was inspired by the malted ice cream at Herrell's in Massachusetts. They were doing smush-ins long before anyone else, and it was there that Anne first tried malted vanilla ice cream with Heath bar pieces mixed in. It was love at first bite!

AT A GLANCE

| TECHNIQUE: | SPECIAL EQUIPMENT: | CHILLING TIME: | SHELF LIFE: |
|---|---|---|---|
| Ice cream (page 12) | Ice cream machine | 2 hours or overnight | 1 week |

5 large egg yolks

1/2 cup malted milk powder (such as Carnation)

1 3/4 cup heavy cream

3/4 cup 1% or 2% milk

1/2 cup sugar

1/4 teaspoon kosher salt

2 ounces milk chocolate, finely chopped or grated (1/3 cup), or make chips (page 182) using 1 teaspoon oil

1 teaspoon vanilla extract

1/2 cup chopped Peanut Brittle (page 131), in 1/8-inch pieces

## MAKE THE BASE

1. In a medium heatproof bowl, whisk the yolks just to break them up, then whisk in the malted milk powder. Set aside.

2. In a heavy nonreactive saucepan, stir together the cream, milk, sugar, and salt and put the pan over medium-high heat. When the mixture approaches a bare simmer, reduce the heat to medium.

3. Carefully scoop out about 1/2 cup of the hot cream mixture and, whisking the eggs constantly, add the cream to the bowl with the egg yolks. Repeat, adding another 1/2 cup of the hot cream to the bowl with the yolks. Using a heatproof rubber spatula, stir the cream in the saucepan as you slowly pour the egg-and-cream mixture from the bowl into the pan.

4. Cook the mixture carefully over medium heat, stirring constantly, until it is thickened, coats the back of a spatula, and holds a clear path when you run your finger across the spatula, 1 to 2 minutes longer.

5. Strain the base through a fine-mesh strainer into a clean container. Set the container into an ice-water bath, wash your spatula, and use it to stir the base occasionally until it is cool. Remove the container from the ice-water bath, cover with plastic wrap, and refrigerate the base for at least 2 hours or overnight.

## FREEZE THE ICE CREAM

6. Add the vanilla to the chilled base and stir until blended.

7. Freeze in your ice cream machine according to the manufacturer's instructions and put the container you'll use to store the ice cream into the freezer. Add the milk chocolate and the peanut brittle in the last minute or so of churning, or fold them in by hand after the ice cream comes out of the machine. Enjoy right away or, for a firmer ice cream, transfer to a container and freeze for at least 4 hours.

# MAPLE WALNUT ICE CREAM

Makes about 1 quart

If there's one ice cream flavor that tastes like fall, this is it! Rich maple syrup and walnuts are the perfect pairing of toasty flavors and complementary textures. Pile a couple of scoops on top of pancakes for a decadent breakfast or dessert.

Use grade B maple syrup, preferably organic, if you can—it has a more intense flavor than the regular amber variety.

## AT A GLANCE

| TECHNIQUE: | SPECIAL EQUIPMENT: | CHILLING TIME: | SHELF LIFE: |
|---|---|---|---|
| Ice cream (page 12) | Ice cream machine | 2 hours or overnight | 1 week |

5 large egg yolks

3/4 cup maple syrup (preferably grade B, organic)

1 3/4 cups heavy cream

3/4 cup 1% or 2% milk

1/4 teaspoon kosher salt

1/2 cup chopped toasted walnuts (see page 114)

### MAKE THE BASE

1. In a medium heatproof bowl, whisk the yolks just to break them up, then whisk in half of the maple syrup (about 6 tablespoons). Set aside.

2. In a heavy nonreactive saucepan, stir together the cream, milk, salt, and the remaining maple syrup (about 6 tablespoons) and put the pan over medium-high heat. When the mixture approaches a bare simmer, reduce the heat to medium.

3. Carefully scoop out about 1/2 cup of the hot cream mixture and, whisking the eggs constantly, add the cream to the bowl with the egg yolks. Repeat, adding another 1/2 cup of the hot cream to the bowl with the yolks. Using a heatproof rubber spatula, stir the cream in the saucepan as you slowly pour the egg-and-cream mixture from the bowl into the pan.

4. Cook the mixture carefully over medium heat, stirring constantly, until it is thickened, coats the back of a spatula, and holds a clear path when you run your finger across the spatula, 1 to 2 minutes longer.

5. Strain the base through a fine-mesh strainer into a clean container. Set the container into an ice-water bath, wash your spatula, and use it to stir the base occasionally until it is cool. Remove the container from the ice-water bath, cover with plastic wrap, and refrigerate the base for at least 2 hours or overnight.

### FREEZE THE ICE CREAM

6. Freeze in your ice cream machine according to the manufacturer's instructions. While the ice cream is churning, put the container you'll use to store the ice cream into the freezer. Add the walnuts in the last minute or so of churning, or fold them in by hand after transferring the ice cream to a chilled container. Enjoy right away or, for a firmer ice cream, freeze for at least 4 hours.

# MEXICAN WEDDING COOKIES

Makes about 2 dozen cookies

We have been making these cookies—the perfect accompaniment to a scoop of ice cream—since we first worked together at 42 Degrees. To give the cookies a nice crunch, we roll the shaped dough in granulated sugar. Then, after baking, we give them a snowy coating of powdered sugar.

**AT A GLANCE** ·····································································

CHILLING TIME: 1 to 2 hours or up to overnight          SHELF LIFE: 1 week

## FOR THE DOUGH

1 cup (8 ounces) cold unsalted butter, cut into
    ¹/₂-inch cubes

1 cup (4¹/₂ ounces) unbleached all-purpose flour

1 cup (4¹/₂ ounces) cake flour

¹/₂ cup powdered sugar, measured then sifted

¹/₂ cup chopped toasted pecans (see page 114)

¹/₂ teaspoon pure vanilla extract

¹/₄ teaspoon kosher salt

## FOR ROLLING

About ¹/₃ cup granulated sugar

About ¹/₂ cup powdered sugar

### MAKE THE DOUGH AND CHILL

1.  Combine all the dough ingredients in the bowl of a stand mixer with the paddle attachment.

2.  Mix on low speed at first, and then increase to medium-low speed and continue mixing until the dough is smooth and just comes together in a solid mass, about 1¹/₂ minutes. Do not mix beyond this point or the cookies will be tough.

3.  Cover the bowl with plastic wrap and chill in the refrigerator until firm, 1 to 2 hours or up to overnight.

### BAKE THE COOKIES

4.  When you're ready to bake, position racks in the top and bottom thirds of the oven and preheat the oven to 350°F. Line two baking sheets with parchment paper or nonstick mats.

5.  Scoop up 1¹/₂ tablespoons of dough and form the dough into a ball. Repeat until all the dough has been shaped. Roll the balls in the granulated sugar and arrange them 1¹/₂ inches apart on the baking sheets.

6.  Bake for 9 minutes, then rotate the sheets top to bottom and front to back. Continue to bake until the cookies are firm to the touch and golden brown on the bottom edge, 6 to 9 minutes longer.

    Let cool on the baking sheets. Once the cookies have cooled, roll them in the powdered sugar. Store in an airtight container.

> **MAKE IT YOUR OWN**
> * You can use any type of nut you like. Almonds and walnuts are really tasty, or you can try the Spiced Pecans on page 132.
> * Add ¹/₂ cup finely chopped bittersweet chocolate along with the other ingredients.

Top and center: Almond Toffee (page 68); bottom: Peanut Brittle

# PEANUT BRITTLE

Makes about 3 cups of 1- to 2-inch pieces

Peanut brittle is truly an indispensable ingredient for us at Bi-Rite Creamery. We break it into large pieces and sell it as a candy around the holidays, but we also chop it finely and use it year-round in ice cream and buttercream frostings. It can be used to add a little extra sweetness and crunch to just about any baking recipe. It is important to use raw peanuts in this recipe; toasted nuts will overcook during the candymaking process.

## AT A GLANCE

**SPECIAL EQUIPMENT:** Candy thermometer   **COOLING TIME:** 1 hour   **SHELF LIFE:** Up to 2 weeks

Nonstick cooking spray (optional)

1 cup sugar

$1/2$ cup water

$1/2$ cup tapioca syrup or corn syrup

$1/4$ teaspoon kosher salt

$1^1/2$ cups raw shelled peanuts, papery skins removed if necessary

$1/8$ teaspoon baking soda

$1^1/2$ teaspoons unsalted butter

1. Line a large rimmed baking sheet with parchment paper or a nonstick mat, or spray with nonstick spray. Set aside.

2. Combine the sugar, water, tapioca syrup, and salt in a small, heavy nonreactive saucepan and attach a candy thermometer. Put the pan over medium heat and cook without stirring until the mixture reaches 280°F, also known as the "soft crack" stage, 20 to 25 minutes.

   **TIP:** *Don't walk away from the pan, especially once it reaches around 250°F, when the mixture becomes more likely to burn.*

3. Remove the thermometer. Stir in the peanuts and continue to stir frequently as the peanuts toast and the syrup browns. When the peanuts are toasted and a golden color and the syrup is a mahogany brown (about

5 minutes longer), remove from the heat. Carefully stir in the baking soda and, once the mixture is blended, stir in the butter.

4. Pour onto the prepared baking sheet and use a heatproof spatula to spread the peanuts in a single even layer about $1/4$ inch thick. (Work quickly before the brittle hardens, but be careful—it's extremely hot!)

5. Let cool to room temperature, about 1 hour. If the top of the brittle looks or feels a little greasy, just blot it with a paper towel. Once cool, break into chunks or chop into $1/8$- to $1/4$-inch pieces and store in an airtight container.

**NOTE:** This is a candy recipe, which means that timing is of the essence. For the best results, read through the entire recipe, measure out all of your ingredients, and set out the necessary equipment before you fire up the stove. A candy thermometer is essential.

**MAKE IT YOUR OWN**

* Any kind of nut would work in this recipe, but it is important to use untoasted nuts. If you were to start with already-toasted nuts, they would likely burn in the process.

# SPICED PECANS

Makes 2 cups

Whereas many spiced nuts feature a light candylike coating of sugar, ours have a unique crumbly/crunchy texture thanks to the mixture of brown sugar and butter that melts together during baking and helps the spices adhere to the nuts. Use these as an ice cream topping, for snacking, and in just about any recipe that calls for nuts.

AT A GLANCE • • • • • • • • • • • • • • • • • • • • • • • • • • • • • • • • • • • • • • • • • • • • • • • •

SHELF LIFE: 1 week

• • • • • • • • • • • • • • • • • • • • • • • • • • • • • • • • • • • • • • • • • • • • • • • • • • • • • • • •

1/4 cup (2 ounces) unsalted butter, melted

1/4 cup packed light or dark brown sugar

1 tablespoon ground cinnamon

1 1/2 teaspoons ground ginger

1 1/2 teaspoons pure vanilla extract

1/4 teaspoon kosher salt

1/8 teaspoon ground cloves

2 cups pecan pieces

1. Position a rack in the center of the oven and preheat the oven to 350°F.
2. In a medium bowl, combine all of the ingredients except the pecans and mix well. Add the nuts and toss until they are thoroughly coated in the butter mixture. Transfer to a rimmed baking sheet and spread in a single layer.
3. Bake for 6 minutes, stir, and bake for another 6 to 9 minutes, or until fragrant and the nuts are golden brown.
4. Remove from the oven and let cool on the baking sheet, stirring occasionally to break up the clumps (they tend to stick together as they cool). It is nice, however, to have some clumps, as they are super-tasty to toss in your mouth!

    Store in an airtight container.

# RODNEY'S GRANOLA

Makes about 12 cups

This recipe came from one of our former bakers and is a favorite topping for our soft-serve ice creams. It's crunchy, nutty, and has the right amount of chew from the dried fruit. It is also perfect with fruit and milk or yogurt for breakfast. Anne has some every morning!

Feel free to substitute other nuts or dried fruits, like chopped dried apricots or dried cherries, to suit your taste. We sprinkle a little Maldon salt over the mixture right before it goes in the oven—it gives the granola a little extra salty crunch—but it's not necessary.

### AT A GLANCE

Cooling time: 1 hour

SHELF LIFE: Up to 4 weeks

4 cups rolled oats (not instant)

1 cup coarsely chopped raw almonds

3/4 cup unsweetened large coconut flakes (aka coconut chips)

1/4 cup flax seeds

1/4 cup sunflower seeds

1 teaspoon kosher salt

3/4 cup packed light or dark brown sugar

1/4 cup plus 2 tablespoons maple syrup (preferably grade B, organic)

1/4 cup honey

5 tablespoons (2 1/2 ounces) unsalted butter

1 tablespoon pure vanilla extract

1 cup packed raisins

1. Position a rack in the center of the oven and preheat the oven to 300°F.

2. In a large bowl, combine the oats, almonds, coconut, flax and sunflower seeds, and salt.

3. Combine the brown sugar, maple syrup, honey, butter, and vanilla in a small saucepan and put the pan over medium heat. Cook, stirring, until the butter is melted and the sugar is dissolved, about 5 minutes. Pour over the dry ingredients and mix until everything is well coated.

4. Spread on a rimmed baking sheet, press to an even thickness, and bake for 30 minutes. Stir the granola and bake for another 15 to 20 minutes, or until golden brown.

   Let cool completely on the baking sheet. Stir in the raisins and transfer to an airtight container. Store at room temperature.

# BERRIES

OUR BERRY ICE CREAMS, SORBETS, AND POPS—especially our Balsamic Strawberry Ice Cream (page 138)—are always in demand, but berries are only in season for about half the year. When they aren't in season, we don't make those recipes. Our guests are sometimes disappointed that their favorite flavor isn't available. However, we use this as an opportunity to talk about the seasonal nature of our products; we want people to understand that when fruits are in season, they taste their best and result in better tasting ice cream and sorbet. We make everything from scratch, use only fresh (not frozen) ingredients, and only when they're truly in season. Ultimately, the proof is in the pudding: our strawberry ice cream is so good *because* we only use ripe, in-season berries. If we made them with imported, frozen, or not-quite-ripe berries, it just wouldn't be the same. It takes only one taste to understand what a difference it makes.

Berries, like any fruit, can be tricky to use in ice cream. Because of their high water content, they often lead to an icy final product. To counteract this, we always cook down our fruit to remove excess water, resulting in a purée that is more concentrated in flavor. This also ensures that the fruit blends evenly into the base, producing a creamy texture with rich flavor. Resist the temptation to add uncooked fruit to ice cream. When frozen, the fruit becomes rock-hard pieces that are an unpleasant contrast to the creaminess of ice cream.

The treatment for fruit is different when making sorbets and ice pops. The fruit is always pureed, but generally not cooked down, because the water content is essential for making these types of frozen desserts. Whole berries can be a fun garnish in ice pops as well; see the recipe for Lime-Blackberry Ice Pops (page 146; pictured opposite), which feature whole blackberries. They do freeze into little nuggets, but they're so beautiful that we use them anyway.

If you're really set on serving whole berries with your ice cream or sorbet, your best bet is to use them as a topping.

## BUYING AND USING BERRIES

Take it from us: for the best possible flavor, buy berries from a local grower and buy them only when they're in season (generally summer, but it depends on where you live and the type of berry). Whether you're using strawberries, blackberries, blueberries, or raspberries, it's especially important to go organic; conventional berries are heavily sprayed with herbicides and pesticides, but organic ones are free of these chemicals.

Berries do not ripen once picked, so look for deep, even color and taste a few to make sure they're as good as they should be. Early season strawberries often have white "shoulders" around the leaves, and their flavor doesn't compare to the fully red ones that come later

**Strawberries:** pint (2 cups)
or quart (4 cups)
**Raspberries:** half pint (1 cup)
**Blackberries:** half pint (1 cup)
or pint (2 cups)
**Blueberries:** varies

in the season. Examine the berries carefully (even looking at the sides and underside of the basket) to make sure they're dry and show no signs of mold or deterioration.

Smaller berries are usually better because they are more flavorful than larger ones. Just think about how flavorful tiny wild blueberries and strawberries are versus giant commercially grown ones. Some of that size difference is due to overwatering by growers, which produces bigger but less flavorful fruit.

Especially when they're ripe, berries are very perishable and have a short shelf life. Buy them as close as possible to the time you want to use them (no more than a day ahead),

and refrigerate them if not using them that same day.

Berries will quickly deteriorate and develop mold after coming in contact with water, so wash them just before you are ready to use them, and wash only as many as you will use right away. (One benefit of using organic berries is that you can sometimes get away without washing them.) If and when you wash your berries, do it gently and properly—simply rinsing berries does not do the trick. Instead, submerge the berries in a large bowl of cold water, allow time for the sand and grit to drop to the bottom, and then gently lift them out with your hands. Repeat as needed until all the sand and grit are gone. Drain in a colander, in the basket they were packed in, or on a towel-lined baking sheet.

**TIP:** *If you buy more berries than you can use within a day or two, wash and dry them well, then spread them on a rimmed baking sheet, freeze, and transfer to a zip-top bag. Frozen strawberries are great for making quick compotes and sauces; smaller berries can be added directly into any muffin or pancake batter.*

# BALSAMIC STRAWBERRY ICE CREAM

Makes about 1 quart | Pictured on page 4

In the United States, peanut butter and jelly are considered a perfect match. In Italy, it's the same thing with strawberries and balsamic vinegar, a classic combination that makes a simple, refreshing dessert. If you've never had this stellar pairing, give our frozen version a shot. The vinegar is subtle and adds depth to the bright sweetness of the strawberries. We add it in two stages (with the cooking berries and just before churning) for an even more complex flavor.

## AT A GLANCE

| TECHNIQUE: | SPECIAL EQUIPMENT: | CHILLING TIME: | SHELF LIFE: |
|---|---|---|---|
| Ice cream (page 12) | Ice cream machine | 2 hours or overnight | 1 week |

### FOR THE STRAWBERRY PURÉE

1¹/₂ pints strawberries (3 cups), preferably organic, hulled and halved or quartered

2¹/₂ tablespoons sugar

2 teaspoons balsamic vinegar

### FOR THE BASE

5 large egg yolks

¹/₂ cup sugar

1³/₄ cups heavy cream

³/₄ cup 1% or 2% milk

¹/₄ teaspoon kosher salt

2 teaspoons balsamic vinegar

### COOK THE BERRIES

1. Combine the berries with the 2¹/₂ tablespoons sugar and 2 teaspoons vinegar in a large nonreactive skillet. Put the skillet over medium heat and cook, stirring frequently, until the strawberries are soft and the liquid they release has reduced somewhat, 6 to 8 minutes.

2. Let cool slightly, then transfer the berries and their juice to a blender or food processor. Purée until smooth and refrigerate until ready to use.

### MAKE THE BASE

3. In a medium heatproof bowl, whisk the yolks just to break them up, then whisk in half of sugar (¹/₄ cup). Set aside.

4. In a heavy nonreactive saucepan, stir together the cream, milk, salt, and the remaining sugar (¹/₄ cup) and put the pan over medium-high heat. When the mixture approaches a bare simmer, reduce the heat to medium.

5. Carefully scoop out about ¹/₂ cup of the hot cream mixture and, whisking the eggs constantly, add the cream to the bowl with the egg yolks. Repeat, adding another ¹/₂ cup of the hot cream to the bowl with the yolks. Using a heatproof rubber spatula, stir the cream in the saucepan as you slowly pour the egg-and-cream mixture from the bowl into the pan.

6. Cook the mixture carefully over medium heat, stirring constantly, until it is thickened, coats the back of a spatula, and holds a clear path when you run your finger across the spatula, 1 to 2 minutes longer.

7. Strain the base through a fine-mesh strainer into a clean container. Set the container into an ice-water bath, wash your spatula, and use

it to stir the base occasionally until it is cool. Remove from the ice-water bath, cover with plastic wrap, and refrigerate the base for at least 2 hours or overnight.

## FREEZE THE ICE CREAM

8. Whisk the strawberry purée and the remaining 2 teaspoons vinegar into the chilled base.
9. Freeze in your ice cream machine according to the manufacturer's instructions. While the ice cream is churning, put the container you'll use to store the ice cream into the freezer. Enjoy right away or, for a firmer ice cream, transfer to the chilled container and freeze for at least 4 hours.

> **SERVE IT WITH . . .**
> ❈ Crème Fraîche Ice cream (page 38), Honey Lavender Ice Cream (page 180), or Chocolate Ice Cream (page 78)
> ❈ Shortbread (page 44) or Brown Sugar Graham Crackers (page 66)
> ❈ Sliced Strawberry Topping (page 149)
> ❈ Vanilla (page 35) and Chocolate (page 78) ice creams and a banana, sliced lengthwise, for a classic banana split

Ice cream cake made with Great Yellow Cake (page 42), Balsamic Strawberry Ice Cream, Whipped Cream (page 51), and Sliced Strawberry Topping (page 149)

Ice cream pie with White Chocolate Raspberry Swirl Ice Cream, Shortbread piecrust (page 44), and Raspberry Swirl Sauce (page 142)

# WHITE CHOCOLATE RASPBERRY SWIRL ICE CREAM

Makes about 1 quart

Everyone who works at the Creamery calls this ice cream "Magic of the '80s." The name came about thanks to a not-so-favorable review on Yelp, in which the reviewer derided the combination of white chocolate and raspberries for being "very '80s." True, the combination was popular back then, but for good reason: the tartness of the raspberries perfectly offsets the creaminess of the white chocolate. The guest eventually took down the review, began dating one of our bakers (they are now engaged!), and now enjoys all the flavors of ice cream (even this one) with great regularity.

## AT A GLANCE

| TECHNIQUE: | SPECIAL EQUIPMENT: | CHILLING TIME: | SHELF LIFE: |
|---|---|---|---|
| Ice cream (page 12) | Ice cream machine | 2 hours or overnight | 1 week |

5 large egg yolks

1/4 cup sugar

5 ounces white chocolate, finely chopped (1 1/4 cups)

2 cups heavy cream

3/4 cup whole milk

1/4 teaspoon kosher salt

1/4 teaspoon pure vanilla extract

1/2 cup Raspberry Swirl Sauce (page 142)

### MAKE THE BASE

1. In a medium heatproof bowl, whisk the yolks just to break them up, then whisk in half of the sugar (2 tablespoons). Set aside. Put the chopped chocolate in another medium heatproof bowl and set that aside as well.

2. In a heavy nonreactive saucepan, stir together the cream, milk, salt, and the remaining sugar (2 tablespoons) and put the pan over medium-high heat. When the mixture approaches a bare simmer, reduce the heat to medium.

3. Carefully scoop out about 1/2 cup of the hot cream mixture and, whisking the eggs constantly, add the cream to the bowl with the egg yolks. Repeat, adding another 1/2 cup of the hot cream to the bowl with the yolks. Using a heatproof rubber spatula, stir the cream in the saucepan as you slowly pour the egg-and-cream mixture from the bowl into the pan.

4. Cook the mixture carefully over medium heat, stirring constantly, until it is thickened, coats the back of a spatula, and holds a clear path when you run your finger across the spatula, 1 to 2 minutes longer.

5. Strain the base through a fine-mesh strainer into the bowl with the white chocolate and whisk to combine. Set the container into an ice-water bath, wash your spatula, and use it to stir the base occasionally until it is cool. Remove the container from the ice-water bath, cover with plastic wrap, and refrigerate the base for at least 2 hours or overnight.

CONTINUED

FREEZE THE ICE CREAM

6. Whisk the vanilla into the chilled base.

7. Freeze in your ice cream machine according to the manufacturer's instructions. While the ice cream is churning, put the container you'll use to store the ice cream into the freezer.

8. As you transfer the ice cream to the storage container, drizzle in some raspberry purée after every few spoonfuls. When all the ice cream is in the container, use a chopstick or butter knife to gently swirl the mixture. Enjoy right away or, for a firmer ice cream, freeze for at least 4 hours.

**MAKE IT YOUR OWN**
* Add finely chopped white chocolate just as the ice cream finishes churning and before incorporating the raspberry swirl.

**SERVE IT WITH . . .**
* Balsamic Strawberry Ice Cream (page 138) or Blackberry Ice Cream (opposite)
* Hot Fudge Sauce (page 93)
* Chopped toasted almonds (see page 114)

# RASPBERRY SWIRL SAUCE

Makes about ¹/₂ cup | Pictured on page 140

We use this primarily as a component of our White Chocolate Raspberry Swirl Ice Cream (page 141), but it also makes a lovely topping for ice cream sundaes, cakes, or pies.

**AT A GLANCE** • • • • • • • • • • • • • • • • • • • • • • • • • • • • • • • • • • • • • • •

CHILLING TIME: 1 hour if swirling into ice cream          SHELF LIFE: 1 week

• • • • • • • • • • • • • • • • • • • • • • • • • • • • • • • • • • • • • • • • • • • • • • • •

2 half-pint baskets raspberries (2 cups), preferably organic

¹/₃ cup sugar

1. Combine the raspberries and sugar in a small nonreactive saucepan and put the pan over medium-high heat. Cook, stirring frequently, until most of the liquid has evaporated and the mixture has a jammy consistency, about 20 minutes. Reduce the heat to medium as the mixture thickens to prevent scorching.

2. Remove from the heat and let cool for a minute. Transfer to a blender and purée until smooth, being careful to avoid hot splatters. Strain through a fine-mesh strainer into a bowl, pressing on the solids to extract as much purée as possible.

If using as a topping, serve warm or at room temperature; chill well before swirling into ice cream.

**MAKE IT YOUR OWN**
* Use blueberries, blackberries, or strawberries in place of raspberries.

# BLACKBERRY ICE CREAM

Makes about 1 quart | Pictured on page 144 (top scoop)

When blackberries are ripe and fragrant and sitting on your counter, sometimes it's all you can do to resist eating them as is, relishing their juicy perfection. If you have enough self-control to save some to make ice cream, though, you'll be amply rewarded. This ice cream is wonderful sandwiched between our Dark Chocolate Cookies (page 90), or served atop a slice of pound cake with whipped cream.

## AT A GLANCE

| TECHNIQUE: | SPECIAL EQUIPMENT: | CHILLING TIME: | SHELF LIFE: |
| --- | --- | --- | --- |
| Ice cream (page 12) | Ice cream machine | 2 hours or overnight | 1 week |

**FOR THE BLACKBERRY PURÉE**

2 half-pint baskets blackberries (2 cups), preferably organic

1/4 to 1/2 cup sugar, as needed

**FOR THE BASE**

5 large egg yolks

1/2 cup sugar

1 3/4 cups heavy cream

3/4 cup 1% or 2% milk

1/4 teaspoon kosher salt

### COOK THE BERRIES

1. Combine the berries with the sugar, using 1/4 cup if they are very sweet and 1/2 cup if less so, in a small nonreactive saucepan and stir well. Put the pan over medium heat and cook, stirring frequently, until the berries are soft and the liquid they release has reduced somewhat, about 10 minutes.

2. Let cool slightly, then transfer the berries and their juice to a blender or food processor. Purée until smooth. Strain half of the mixture through a fine-mesh strainer into a medium bowl, pressing on the solids to extract as much purée as possible. Discard the solids. Add the unstrained purée to the same bowl and stir once to combine. Cover the bowl and refrigerate.

### MAKE THE BASE

3. In a medium heatproof bowl, whisk the yolks just to break them up, then whisk in half of the sugar (1/4 cup). Set aside.

4. In a heavy nonreactive saucepan, stir together the cream, milk, salt, and the remaining sugar (1/4 cup) and put the pan over medium-high heat. When the mixture approaches a bare simmer, reduce the heat to medium.

5. Carefully scoop out about 1/2 cup of the hot cream mixture and, whisking the eggs constantly, add the cream to the bowl with the egg yolks. Repeat, adding another 1/2 cup of the hot cream to the bowl with the yolks. Using a heatproof rubber spatula, stir the cream in the saucepan as you slowly pour the egg-and-cream mixture from the bowl into the pan.

6. Cook the mixture carefully over medium heat, stirring constantly, until it is thickened, coats the back of a spatula, and holds a clear

CONTINUED

path when you run your finger across the spatula, 1 to 2 minutes longer.

7. Strain the base through a fine-mesh strainer into a clean container. Set the container into an ice-water bath, wash your spatula, and use it to stir the base occasionally until it is cool. Remove the container from the ice-water bath, cover with plastic wrap, and refrigerate the base for at least 2 hours or overnight.

### FREEZE THE ICE CREAM

8. Whisk the blackberry purée into the chilled base.

9. Freeze in your ice cream machine according to the manufacturer's instructions. While the ice cream is churning, put the container you'll use to store the ice cream into the freezer. Enjoy right away or, for a firmer ice cream, transfer to the chilled container and freeze for at least 4 hours.

**MAKE IT YOUR OWN**
* Use raspberries or a combination of blackberries and raspberries.
* Add 1 to 2 tablespoons crème de cassis (black currant liqueur) or bourbon as you whisk the berry purée into the base.

**SERVE IT WITH . . .**
* Buttermilk Ice Cream (page 37) or Honey Lavender Ice Cream (page 180)
* Hot Fudge Sauce (page 93)
* Brown Sugar Graham Crackers (page 66)
* Chopped Marcona almonds

Top scoop: Blackberry Ice Cream; bottom scoop: Cherry Almond Ice Cream (page 117)

# STRAWBERRY ICE POPS

Makes eight 3-ounce ice pops

These pops are a favorite among our younger guests. We keep the ingredients simple but use a trick in the execution: we purée the strawberries and strain out most, but not all, of the seeds and solids. This produces a relatively smooth pop with just enough seeds to make it taste like real strawberries.

## AT A GLANCE

| TECHNIQUE: | SPECIAL EQUIPMENT: | CHILLING TIME: | SHELF LIFE: |
|---|---|---|---|
| Ice Pops (page 20) | Ice pop molds | At least 4 hours | 1 week |

3 pints strawberries (6 cups), preferably organic
1/2 to 3/4 cup 1:1 Simple Syrup (page 18), cooled
1 1/2 tablespoons strained fresh lemon juice
1 teaspoon balsamic vinegar (optional)

### MAKE THE BASE

1. Cut off and discard the tops of the berries and purée in a food processor or blender until smooth.

2. Transfer one-fourth of the mixture to a medium bowl; strain the rest of the purée through a fine-mesh strainer into the bowl, pressing on the solids to extract as much purée as possible.

   Add 1/2 cup of the simple syrup, the lemon juice, and the vinegar if using. Stir until well combined.

3. Taste the base. It should taste just a bit too sweet (once frozen, it will lose some of its sweetness). Add the remaining simple syrup if you need it.

### FREEZE THE POPS

4. Transfer the base to a liquid measuring cup and pour into the ice pop molds. Insert the sticks and freeze until completely solid, about 4 hours. Unmold just before serving.

# LIME-BLACKBERRY ICE POPS

Makes ten 3-ounce ice pops | Pictured on page 137

Ice pops can have a variety of textures and consistencies, depending on what ingredients are in them. Fruit with more pulp creates a slightly softer consistency, whereas citrus juices and other watery bases freeze into something more solid, like these pops do. To us, there's a place for all pops in the spectrum of frozen treats.

This is one of the only instances in which we freeze berries without puréeing them first, and it's purely for visual appeal. A pink hue emanates from the whole blackberries and permeates the rest of the pop, sort of like a watercolor painting. The result is gorgeous! This pop is a favorite of Anne's oldest daughter Zoe.

## AT A GLANCE

| TECHNIQUE: | SPECIAL EQUIPMENT: | CHILLING TIME: | SHELF LIFE: |
|---|---|---|---|
| Ice Pops (page 20) | Ice pop molds | At least 4 hours | 1 week |

1/2 cup plus 2 tablespoons 2:1 Simple Syrup (page 18), cooled

1 cup strained fresh lime juice (from about 8 medium limes)

1 cup water

1/8 teaspoon kosher salt

1 half-pint basket blackberries (1 cup), preferably organic, berries halved if very large

### MAKE THE BASE

1. In a medium bowl, combine 1/2 cup of the simple syrup, the lime juice, water, and salt. Stir until well combined and the salt has dissolved.

2. Taste the base. It should taste just a bit too sweet (once frozen, it will lose some of its sweetness). Add the remaining simple syrup if you need it.

### FREEZE THE ICE POPS

3. Add 4 berries (or berry halves) to each ice pop mold. (Don't add too many or the pops will be too icy. Leave enough room so that you end up with more juice than fruit in each pop.)

4. Transfer the base to a liquid measuring cup and pour into the ice pop molds. Insert the sticks and freeze until completely solid, about 4 hours. Unmold just before serving.

> **MAKE IT YOUR OWN**
> ❋ Use freshly squeezed lemon juice in place of lime juice.
> ❋ Use raspberries in place of blackberries.

# RASPBERRY ICE POPS

Makes ten 3-ounce ice pops

Raspberries are notoriously delicate and perishable, which is why they're usually packed in half-pint containers (any bigger and they will collapse under their own weight). This recipe is the perfect way to preserve raspberries' glory for a little longer. These pops are glossy and saturated with that gorgeous magenta hue.

## AT A GLANCE

| TECHNIQUE: | SPECIAL EQUIPMENT: | CHILLING TIME: | SHELF LIFE: |
|---|---|---|---|
| Ice pops (page 20) | Ice pop molds | At least 4 hours | 1 week |

4 half-pint baskets raspberries (4 cups), preferably organic

$^1/_2$ cup water

$^3/_4$ cup 1:1 Simple Syrup (page 18)

### MAKE THE BASE

1. Combine the berries, water, and $^1/_2$ cup of the simple syrup in a blender or food processor and purée until smooth. Strain $^1/_2$ to $^3/_4$ of the mixture (depending on how many seeds you like in your ice pops) through a fine-mesh strainer into a medium bowl, pressing on the solids to extract as much purée as possible. Discard the seeds and stir in the remaining unstrained purée.

2. Taste the base. It should taste just a bit too sweet (once frozen, it will lose some of its sweetness). Add the remaining simple syrup if you need it.

### FREEZE THE ICE POPS

3. Transfer the base to a liquid measuring cup and pour into the ice pop molds. Insert the sticks and freeze until completely solid, about 4 hours. Unmold just before serving.

# BERRY COMPOTE

Makes about 2 cups

Berry sauces or toppings are often made by cooking the fruit until it softens and starts to break down. The textural effect can be wonderful, but the fresh flavor of the berries is diminished as they cook. Our version has the best of both worlds, featuring fresh whole raspberries bound together by a lightly sweetened purée of uncooked strawberries.

This sauce is best enjoyed the same day it's made.

AT A GLANCE ·····················································································
SHELF LIFE: 1 day
···························································································································

1 pint strawberries (2 cups), preferably organic

1 half-pint basket raspberries (1 cup), preferably organic

¼ cup 1:1 Simple Syrup (page 18)

Water, fresh lemon juice, or framboise, as needed

> **MAKE IT YOUR OWN**
> ❊ You can use blackberries in place of the strawberries or raspberries (halve them in step 2). Do not use blueberries, as they turn an unsightly gray hue when puréed.

1. Trim and discard the tops of the strawberries. Put half of the strawberries in a blender or food processor, along with half of the raspberries. Purée until smooth, then pour through a fine-mesh strainer into a medium bowl, pressing on the solids to extract as much purée as possible.

2. Halve or quarter the remaining strawberries and add them to the purée along with the remaining raspberries and the simple syrup. Toss gently to coat. Serve chilled or at room temperature.

   If the mixture is too thick, thin with a few drops of water, lemon juice, or framboise.

# SLICED STRAWBERRY TOPPING

Makes about 1¹/₂ cups | Pictured on page 139

This topping, designed to showcase the texture of perfectly ripe strawberries, is chunky and light rather than thick and saucy. The optional balsamic vinegar gives it tang and depth.

Make this no more than a few hours ahead of time; any longer and the berries will start to become too mushy.

## AT A GLANCE

WAITING TIME: At least 20 minutes

1 pint strawberries (2 cups), preferably organic

2 to 3 tablespoons sugar

¹/₄ teaspoon pure vanilla extract or seeds from ¹/₂ vanilla bean

1 teaspoon balsamic vinegar (optional)

**MAKE IT YOUR OWN**

❉ Use blackberries or raspberries in place of strawberries (halve the blackberries; the raspberries can be left whole).

❉ Substitute champagne vinegar for the balsamic vinegar.

1. Trim and discard the tops of the berries, then quarter the berries lengthwise and transfer to a medium bowl. Sprinkle with the sugar (the amount needed will depend on the sweetness of the berries), vanilla, and balsamic (if using) and toss gently to combine.

2. Let stand at least 20 minutes at room temperature to allow the sugar to dissolve. Serve chilled or at room temperature; the flavors will be stronger at room temperature.

# BLUEBERRY-LEMON SAUCE

Makes about 1¼ cups

This tart and tangy sauce, which features a combination of cooked and raw blueberries, couldn't be simpler. The cooked ones contribute an intense jammy flavor, and the fresh ones give that satisfying "pop" when you bite into them.

AT A GLANCE ••••••••••••••••••••••••••••••••••••••••••••••••••••••••••••••••••••••••••

SPECIAL EQUIPMENT: Microplane or other rasp grater        SHELF LIFE: 1 week
••••••••••••••••••••••••••••••••••••••••••••••••••••••••••••••••••••••••••••••••••••••••

1 lemon
1 pint (2 cups) blueberries, preferably organic
⅓ cup sugar

1. Working over a small nonreactive saucepan, finely grate the zest from the lemon into the pan. Juice the lemon into a bowl and set aside.

2. Add 1½ cups of the blueberries and the sugar to the pan and put over medium-high heat. Cook until most of the berries have popped and the juice they release has thickened slightly, 6 to 8 minutes.

3. Remove from the heat and stir in the remaining ½ cup of berries and the lemon juice.

4. Serve warm or at room temperature, or transfer to a container and refrigerate until ready to use. Refrigerated, the sauce will keep for up to a week, but it's best the same day it's made.

Berry sundae with Crème Fraîche Ice Cream
(page 38) and Blueberry-Lemon Sauce with
Lemon Gingersnaps (page 169)

# CITRUS

CITRUS—AND SPECIFICALLY LEMON—was the subject of one of our first triumphs in ice cream experimentation. From the very beginning we were able to make good lemon ice cream. That wasn't the problem. Our problem was that we wanted to make *really lemony* ice cream. As you might guess, lemon is highly acidic, and even a moderate quantity of it will cause cream and milk to curdle. Whenever we tried upping our normal quantity of lemon juice in the ice cream recipe, the base couldn't handle the extra acid. We tried using extra lemon zest, but that didn't give use the tartness we wanted. After much trial and error, we finally figured out that lemon curd was the answer. Curd is essentially lemon juice that's stabilized in an egg custard, which keeps it from coagulating the ice cream base. At last we got the mouth-puckering, extra-lemony flavor we desired.

## BUYING AND USING CITRUS

Citrus really shines in the wintertime, when it is abundant and at its best. It is worth seeking out interesting and unique varietals of citrus, especially cara cara oranges, moro blood oranges, pixie tangerines, bergamots, ruby grapefruits, and sweet limes.

Choose citrus fruits that have shiny, taut skin and are heavy for their size. Keep them at room temperature if using within a few days, or refrigerate them in a plastic bag for longer storage.

**TIP:** *Although they are both called "lemons," Eureka or Lisbon lemons and Meyer lemons are actually pretty different from one another. Eurekas or Lisbons are the standard variety that you're likely to find at the grocery store. Meyer lemons are a cross between a lemon and a sweet orange; they're more aromatic, sweeter, and less acidic than standard lemons. The two types are more or less interchangeable, although you won't get as much of that true lemony tartness by using only Meyer lemons in a recipe. For that reason, several of the* recipes in this chapter (primarily those calling for more than a couple of tablespoons of lemon juice) recommend that at least a portion of the juice come from Eureka or Lisbon lemons.

A handheld lever-style citrus press (the kind you often see bartenders use) is our tool of choice for squeezing citrus. It's fast, it gives the maximum yield of juice, and the squeezing action helps to release the essential oils in the zest. Metal ones are sturdiest, but make sure they're coated to prevent discoloration of the juice. A reamer-style juicer is the second best option. It doesn't extract the essential oils the way the lever style juicer does, and it can start to feel tedious if you need a large quantity of juice. However, it certainly gets the job done.

The outside of citrus fruits contains lots of flavor in the form of the zest. This is the thinnest outer layer of the skin containing the essential oils. These aromatic oils have a slightly floral quality not found in the juice itself. Using both the zest and the juice gives a fuller, deeper citrus flavor to whatever you're making. For that reason, we almost always recommend using both the zest and the juice (even if the zest eventually gets strained out). A Microplane rasp grater is the best tool for grating fine tendrils of zest from citrus fruit. The flat, shallow teeth grab all the flavorful zest you want and none of the bitter pith you don't want. Be sure to use organically grown citrus if you plan to use the zest. Even a thorough washing doesn't remove all of the chemical residue found on sprayed fruit.

You can often substitute one type of citrus for another depending on what's available. If you make a substitution in a recipe, however, try to match the sweetness and acidity of whatever type of citrus the recipe calls for. Otherwise the final product might be too sweet or too sour.

## TIPS FOR MAXIMIZING CITRUS FLAVOR

**Store citrus properly.** If you're going to use the fruit within a few days, leaving it in a bowl at room temperature is fine. However, much longer than that and the skin starts to dry out and become leathery—not exactly optimal for zesting! For longer storage, put the fruit in a plastic bag in the refrigerator.

**Never use aluminum** when working with citrus. Aluminum is a reactive metal, which means it causes acidic foods to discolor. Stainless steel or glass are your best bets if you need a heatproof container; otherwise, plastic is fine.

**Zest first, then juice.** It's a lot easier to juice a zested lemon than it is to zest a juiced one! It isn't impossible to do the latter, but you're more likely to scrape your knuckles in the process.

## LEMON AND LIME YIELDS

1 medium (4½-ounce) lemon =
3 tablespoons juice +
1 lightly packed tablespoon
finely grated zest

1 medium (3¼-ounce) lime =
2 tablespoons juice* +
2 lightly packed teaspoons
finely grated zest

*Limes can vary greatly in the amount of juice they will yield. Buying the heaviest ones is the best way to ensure you get enough juice, but it never hurts to buy a few extras.

**Grate directly over the bowl** you'll be adding the zest to. Each time you draw the citrus peel over the grater, a fine mist of essential oils goes flying into the air. Working over the mixing bowl helps you capture as much of that oil as possible.

**Let citrus come to room temperature** before juicing. The fruit will be more malleable and easier to squeeze that way.

**Roll citrus on the counter** before juicing. This also helps soften the fruit and "pre-release" the juice for squeezing.

# MEYER LEMON ICE CREAM

Makes about 1 quart | Pictured on page 29

It may seem like a lot of extra work to make lemon curd solely for the purpose of using it in ice cream, but it really is the best way to maximize lemony flavor without sacrificing texture.

The curd in this recipe is similar to the lemon curd on page 171, but here we omit the butter; in ice cream, butter would be too rich and would mask the citrus flavor. You will have a little leftover curd, which you can use as a topping on ice cream, dollop onto scones, or spread on anything you want spiked with rich lemony flavor. You can make this recipe with all Eureka lemons for a tarter version of this ice cream.

## AT A GLANCE

| TECHNIQUE: | SPECIAL EQUIPMENT: | CHILLING TIME: | SHELF LIFE: |
|---|---|---|---|
| Ice cream (page 12) | Ice cream machine and Microplane or other rasp grater | 2 hours or overnight | 1 week |

**FOR THE CURD**

2 Meyer lemons and 1 Eureka lemon

7 large egg yolks

³/₄ cup sugar

**FOR THE ICE CREAM**

5 large egg yolks

¹/₂ cup sugar

1³/₄ cups heavy cream

³/₄ cup 1% or 2% milk

¹/₄ teaspoon kosher salt

### MAKE THE LEMON CURD

1. Put about 2 inches of water in the bottom of a double boiler or medium saucepan and bring to a simmer over medium-high heat. If you are using a gas stove, make sure the flames are not coming up around the pan to prevent the curd from scorching.

2. Finely grate the zest from the lemons into the top of the double boiler or the non-reactive bowl you will be using to make your curd (you should have about 3 tablespoons). Juice the lemons and measure out ¹/₂ cup juice (if using a mix of lemon types, make sure at least one-third of the juice is from Eureka lemons). Save the rest of the juice for another use.

3. Whisk the yolks into the zest, then whisk in the ¾ cup sugar. Add the lemon juice and whisk to blend. Put the double boiler insert or bowl over but not touching the simmering water. Cook, whisking frequently until the mixture is thick and puddinglike and leaves a trail when stirred, about 10 minutes. (Check the water level periodically and add more if it threatens to boil away.)

4. When the curd has thickened, remove from the heat and pour through a fine-mesh strainer into a bowl. (Use a spatula to gently press the curd through the strainer.) Lay plastic wrap directly on the surface of the curd and refrigerate until completely chilled, about 2 hours. Meanwhile, make the ice cream base (it will need to chill for 2 hours, too).

## MAKE THE ICE CREAM BASE

5. In a medium heatproof bowl, whisk the yolks just to break them up, then whisk in half of the sugar (¼ cup). Set aside.

6. In a heavy nonreactive saucepan, combine the cream, milk, salt, and the remaining sugar (¼ cup) and put the pan over medium-high heat. When the mixture approaches a bare simmer, reduce the heat to medium.

7. Carefully scoop out about ½ cup of the hot cream mixture and, whisking the eggs constantly, add the cream to the bowl with the egg yolks. Repeat, adding another ½ cup of the hot cream to the bowl with the yolks. Using a heatproof rubber spatula, stir the cream in the saucepan as you slowly pour the egg-and-cream mixture from the bowl into the pan.

8. Cook the mixture carefully over medium heat, stirring constantly, until it is thickened, coats the back of a spatula, and holds a clear path when you run your finger across the spatula, 1 to 2 minutes longer.

9. Strain the base through a fine-mesh strainer into a clean container. Set the container into an ice-water bath, wash your spatula, and use it to stir the base occasionally until it is cool. Remove the container from the ice-water bath, cover with plastic wrap, and refrigerate the base for at least 2 hours or overnight.

## FREEZE THE ICE CREAM

10. Put ¾ cup of the lemon curd in a medium bowl and whisk in the chilled base a little at a time until smooth. (You won't get as many lumps if you slowly whisk the base into the curd instead of the other way around.)

11. Freeze in your ice cream machine according to the manufacturer's instructions. While the ice cream is churning, put the container you'll use to store the ice cream into the freezer. Enjoy right away or, for a firmer ice cream, transfer to the chilled container and freeze for at least 4 hours.

---

**SERVE IT WITH . . .**
* Lemon Gingersnaps (page 169) for an ice cream sandwich
* Shortbread piecrust (page 44) and Meringue (page 50) to make a frozen lemon meringue pie

# ORANGE-CARDAMOM ICE CREAM

Makes about 1 quart

We love to make this in the winter, when citrus is really doing its thing. This ice cream is unique in that it uses only the zest from the orange and none of the juice. The result is a delicate, floral citrus flavor that is a nice complement to the aromatic cardamom.

## AT A GLANCE

| TECHNIQUE: | SPECIAL EQUIPMENT: | INFUSING AND CHILLING TIME: | SHELF LIFE: |
|---|---|---|---|
| Ice cream (page 12) | Ice cream machine and Microplane or other rasp grater | 30 minutes, plus 2 hours or overnight | 1 week |

2 tablespoons green cardamom pods

1³/₄ cups heavy cream

³/₄ cup 1% or 2% milk

¹/₂ cup sugar

¹/₄ teaspoon kosher salt

5 large egg yolks

1 large orange

### INFUSE THE MILK/CREAM

1. Put the cardamom in a small skillet and put the pan over medium heat. Toast the pods, stirring frequently, until aromatic, 2 to 3 minutes. Remove from the heat, let cool for a minute, then use a sharp knife to coarsely chop the pods.

   **TIP:** *Cardamom pods have a tendency to fly all over the place when you chop them. To minimize this, use a sharp knife and slow, deliberate motions as you chop. Or you can crush the pods by rocking the bottom of a small sauté pan back and forth over them on a cutting board.*

2. In a heavy nonreactive saucepan, stir together the cardamom, cream, milk, half of the sugar (¹/₄ cup), and the salt.

3. Put the pan over medium-high heat. When the mixture just begins to bubble around the edges, remove from the heat and cover the pan. Let steep for about 30 minutes, or until the cream mixture has a distinct cardamom flavor. (Taste it to monitor the progress; the mixture will become bitter if oversteeped.)

### MAKE THE BASE

4. In a medium heatproof bowl, whisk the yolks just to break them up, then whisk in the remaining sugar (¹/₄ cup). Set aside.

5. Uncover the cream mixture and put the pan over medium-high heat. When the mixture approaches a bare simmer, reduce the heat to medium.

6. Carefully scoop out about ¹/₂ cup of the hot cream mixture and, whisking the eggs constantly, add the cream to the bowl with the egg yolks. Repeat, adding another ¹/₂ cup of the hot cream to the bowl with the yolks. Using a heatproof rubber spatula, stir the cream in the saucepan as you slowly pour the egg-and-cream mixture from the bowl into the pan.

7. Cook the mixture carefully over medium heat, stirring constantly, until it is thickened, coats the back of a spatula, and holds a clear path when you run your finger across the spatula, 1 to 2 minutes longer.

8. Strain the base through a fine-mesh strainer into a clean container. Zest the orange over the warm base and stir to combine. Set the container into an ice-water bath, wash your spatula, and use it to stir the base occasionally until it is cool. Remove the container from the ice-water bath, cover with plastic wrap, and refrigerate the base for at least 2 hours or overnight.

## FREEZE THE ICE CREAM

9. Freeze in your ice cream machine according to the manufacturer's instructions. While the ice cream is churning, put the container you'll use to store the ice cream into the freezer. Enjoy right away or, for a firmer ice cream, transfer to the chilled container and freeze for at least 4 hours.

**MAKE IT YOUR OWN**

❋ Try another variety of orange, such as navel or Valencia. Just make sure it has nice taut skin so that is has a full-flavored zest.

❋ Replace the cardamom with a cinnamon stick, a couple of star anise, or a few Szechuan peppercorns.

❋ Fold chopped toasted pistachios (see page 114) into the finished ice cream.

**SERVE IT WITH . . .**

❋ Earl Grey Ice Cream (page 109) or Crème Fraîche Ice Cream (page 38)

❋ Dark Chocolate Cookies (page 90) to make an ice cream sandwich

# MANDARIN ORANGE OLIVE OIL ICE CREAM

Makes about 1 quart

Extra-virgin olive oil adds a wonderful texture and sublime flavor to this ice cream. We like to use the organic olive oil produced by Etruria, who also make our favorite bergamot olive oil (used in Sam's Sundae, page 79) and mandarin olive oil. You don't have to use a flavored oil; this recipe can be made with any olive oil that you love.

## AT A GLANCE

| TECHNIQUE: | SPECIAL EQUIPMENT: | CHILLING TIME: | SHELF LIFE: |
|---|---|---|---|
| Ice cream (page 12) | Ice cream machine | 2 hours or overnight | 1 week |

5 large egg yolks

3/4 cup sugar

2 cups heavy cream

1 cup 1% or 2% milk

1/4 teaspoon kosher salt

1/4 cup mandarin orange olive oil or other favorite olive oil

### MAKE THE BASE

1. In a medium heatproof bowl, whisk the yolks just to break them up, then whisk in half of the sugar (6 tablespoons). Set aside.

2. In a heavy nonreactive saucepan, stir together the cream, milk, salt, and the remaining sugar (6 tablespoons) and put the pan over medium-high heat. When the mixture approaches a bare simmer, reduce the heat to medium.

3. Carefully scoop out about 1/2 cup of the hot cream mixture and, whisking the eggs constantly, add the cream to the bowl with the egg yolks. Repeat, adding another 1/2 cup of the hot cream to the bowl with the yolks. Using a heatproof rubber spatula, stir the cream in the saucepan as you slowly pour the egg-and-cream mixture from the bowl into the pan.

4. Cook the mixture carefully over medium heat, stirring constantly, until it is thickened, coats the back of a spatula, and holds a clear path when you run your finger across the spatula, 1 to 2 minutes longer.

5. Strain the base through a fine-mesh strainer into a clean container. Set the container into an ice-water bath, wash your spatula, and use it to stir the base occasionally until it is cool. Remove the container from the ice-water bath, cover with plastic wrap, and refrigerate the base for at least 2 hours or overnight.

### FREEZE THE ICE CREAM

6. Whisk the olive oil into the chilled base until well blended.

7. Freeze in your ice cream machine according to the manufacturer's instructions. While the ice cream is churning, put the container you'll use to store the ice cream into the freezer. Enjoy right away or, for a firmer ice cream, transfer to the chilled container and freeze for at least 4 hours.

# PINK GRAPEFRUIT SORBET

Makes about 1 quart | Pictured on page 116

This is a very refreshing, tart sorbet. We call for Meyer lemon juice here simply because its extra sweetness helps balance out the tartness of the grapefruit juice. Feel free to use regular Eureka lemon juice, but you may need to use a little extra simple syrup.

## AT A GLANCE

| TECHNIQUE: | SPECIAL EQUIPMENT: | SHELF LIFE: |
| --- | --- | --- |
| Sorbet (page 17) | Ice cream machine | 1 week |

¹/₄ cup 2:1 Simple Syrup (page 18), cooled

3 cups fresh pink grapefruit juice (from about 6 large grapefruits)

¹/₄ cup tapioca syrup or corn syrup

2 tablespoons strained fresh Meyer lemon juice

¹/₄ teaspoon kosher salt

### MAKE THE BASE

1. In a medium nonreactive bowl, combine 2 tablespoons of the simple syrup, the grapefruit juice, tapioca syrup, lemon juice, and salt. Stir until well combined and the salt is completely dissolved.

2. Taste the base. It should taste just a bit too sweet (once the sorbet is frozen, it will lose some of its sweetness). Add the remaining simple syrup if you need it.

### FREEZE THE SORBET

3. Freeze in your ice cream machine according to the manufacturer's instructions. While the sorbet is churning, put the container you'll use to store the sorbet into the freezer. Enjoy right away or, for a firmer sorbet, transfer to the chilled container and freeze for about 4 hours.

---

**MAKE IT YOUR OWN**

❊ Mix the grapefruit juice with other citrus juices such as blood orange, lemon, and/or tangerine. You can also use regular white grapefruits, but the color won't be quite as pretty and you may need additional simple syrup, since white grapefruits are not as sweet as the pink ones.

**SERVE IT WITH . . .**

❊ Meyer Lemon Ice Cream (page 156) or Tangerine Granita (page 167)

❊ Shortbread (page 44)

# BLOOD ORANGE SORBET

Makes about 1 quart

When they're in season, blood oranges make many appearances at Bi-Rite Creamery. This sorbet is a favorite of ours; it has the perfect balance of acid and sweetness, with a stunning garnet hue to boot.

## AT A GLANCE

| TECHNIQUE: | SPECIAL EQUIPMENT: | SHELF LIFE: |
|---|---|---|
| Sorbet (page 17) | Ice cream machine | 1 week |

¹/₄ cup 2:1 Simple Syrup (page 18), cooled

3¹/₂ cups fresh blood orange juice (from 10 to 12 blood oranges)

¹/₄ cup tapioca syrup or corn syrup

2 tablespoons strained lemon juice

¹/₄ teaspoon kosher salt

### MAKE THE BASE

1.  In a medium nonreactive bowl, combine 2 tablespoons of the simple syrup, the orange juice, tapioca syrup, lemon juice, and salt. Stir until well combined and the salt is completely dissolved.

2.  Taste the base. It should taste just a bit too sweet (once the sorbet is frozen, it will lose some of its sweetness). Add the remaining simple syrup if you need it.

### FREEZE THE SORBET

3.  Freeze in your ice cream machine according to the manufacturer's instructions. While the sorbet is churning, put the container you'll use to store the sorbet into the freezer. Enjoy right away or, for a firmer sorbet, transfer to the chilled container and freeze for about 4 hours.

### MAKE IT YOUR OWN

❋ Use other sweet citrus juices such as mandarin orange, cara cara orange, and/or tangerine. Be sure to adjust the level of simple syrup according to the sweetness of the fruit you are using.

### SERVE IT WITH . . .

❋ Crème Fraîche Ice Cream (page 38)
❋ Dark Chocolate Cookies (page 90)

# TANGERINE ICE POPS

Makes six 3-ounce ice pops

This is wonderful recipe to brighten the winter doldrums. We take advantage of the many varieties of citrus available at Bi-Rite Market and change up the fruit depending on what tastes best. Our favorite combination is a mixture of Page and Satsuma tangerines, but let your taste buds guide you. Use whatever is most flavorful and in season.

We always strain the mixture for the smoothest possible consistency, but feel free to skip this step if you like.

## AT A GLANCE

| TECHNIQUE: | SPECIAL EQUIPMENT: | CHILLING TIME: | SHELF LIFE: |
|---|---|---|---|
| Ice pops (page 20) | Ice pop molds | At least 4 hours | 1 week |

1/2 cup 2:1 Simple Syrup (page 18), cooled

2 cups strained fresh tangerine juice (from about 12 tangerines)

3 tablespoons strained fresh lemon juice

1/8 teaspoon kosher salt

### MAKE THE BASE

1. In a medium nonreactive bowl, combine 6 tablespoons of the simple syrup, the tangerine and lemon juices, and the salt. Stir until well combined and the salt has dissolved.

2. Taste the base. It should taste just a bit too sweet (once frozen, it will lose some of its sweetness). Add the remaining simple syrup if you need it.

### FREEZE THE ICE POPS

3. Strain the base through a mesh strainer into a liquid measuring cup. Pour into ice pop molds, insert the sticks, and freeze until completely solid, about 4 hours. Unmold just before serving.

> **MAKE IT YOUR OWN**
> * Add a few pomegranate seeds to each pop mold. They're like little jewels floating in your pop!

# BLOOD ORANGE ICE POPS

Makes about nine 3-ounce ice pops

**These pops are favorites of ours simply because they're so beautiful.**

## AT A GLANCE

| | | | |
|---|---|---|---|
| **TECHNIQUES:** Ice pops (page 20), segmenting citrus (see below) | **SPECIAL EQUIPMENT:** Ice pop molds | **CHILLING TIME:** At least 4 hours | **SHELF LIFE:** 1 week |

1/2 cup 2:1 Simple Syrup (page 18), cooled

2 1/4 cups fresh blood orange juice (from 6 to 8 blood oranges)

1/8 teaspoon kosher salt

About 30 segments of blood, cara cara, or other variety of orange (see below)

## MAKE THE BASE

1. In a medium nonreactive bowl, combine 6 tablespoons of the simple syrup, the juice, and the salt. Stir until well combined and the salt has dissolved.

2. Taste the base. It should taste just a bit too sweet (once frozen, it will lose some of its sweetness). Add the remaining simple syrup if you need it.

## FREEZE THE ICE POPS

3. Add 2 or 3 orange slices or segments to each ice pop mold. (Don't add too many or the pops will be hard and icy. Leave room so that you end up with more juice than fruit in each pop.)

4. Strain the base through a fine-mesh strainer into a liquid measuring cup. Pour into the ice pop molds, insert the sticks, and freeze until completely solid, about 4 hours. Unmold just before serving.

## HOW TO MAKE CITRUS SEGMENTS

This technique is useful when you want pieces of citrus fruit that are completely free of skin and membranes—perfect for adding to ice pops, topping a sundae, or garnishing a pie.

Slice the top and bottom off the fruit to expose the flesh. Set the fruit with one of the cut sides down on the cutting board. Then, working top to bottom, slice off a thin strip of the peel, removing as much of the white pith as possible. Repeat all the way around until no pith is remaining. Set the fruit on its side. Starting with the topmost segment, make two cuts just inside the membrane on either side of the segment. (For this delicate work, it helps to use a paring knife rather than a chef's knife.) Remove the segment and repeat all the way around.

Tangerine Granita with Vanilla Ice Cream (page 35)

# TANGERINE GRANITA

Makes about 1 quart

You can use just about any kind of orange, tangerine, or mandarin orange juice in this recipe, or even use a mixture of several different kinds.

## AT A GLANCE

TECHNIQUE: Granita (page 18)    CHILLING TIME: About 3 hours    SHELF LIFE: 1 week

1/2 cup 2:1 Simple Syrup (see page 18), cooled

2 1/4 cups strained fresh tangerine juice (from about 14 tangerines)

2 tablespoons strained fresh lemon juice

1/8 teaspoon kosher salt

### MAKE THE BASE

1. In a medium nonreactive bowl, combine 6 tablespoons of the simple syrup, the tangerine and lemon juices, and the salt. Stir until well combined and the salt has dissolved.

2. Taste the base. It should taste just a bit too sweet (once the granita is frozen, it will lose some of its sweetness). Add the remaining simple syrup if you need it.

### FREEZE THE GRANITA

3. Pour the base into an 8- or 9-inch square baking dish or similar shallow pan. Freeze uncovered for 1 hour, or until ice crystals start to form.

4. Stir the mixture with a fork to break up the crystals. Return the baking dish to the freezer and stir every 30 minutes or so to break up the ice crystals as the granita freezes. When the granita is completely frozen (2 1/2 to 3 hours total), it should have a light, feathery texture.

Serve right away or transfer to a container and store in the freezer. Break up the mixture with a fork just before serving.

### MAKE IT YOUR OWN

※ You can use the juice of ruby grapefruits, pomelos, or Meyer lemons in place of tangerine juice. These tarter citrus fruits will require additional sugar, so taste a bit of the base and add more simple syrup if necessary before freezing.

### SERVE IT WITH . . .

※ A glass of champagne to make a mimosa float

※ Vanilla Ice Cream (page 35) or Whipped Cream (page 51)—the bit of rich dairy is a nice counterpoint to the cool citrus

# CANDIED CITRUS ZEST

Makes about thirty 1 by 3-inch strips of zest

This is the perfect thing to make whenever you have a recipe that calls for fresh squeezed citrus juice. Zest the fruit before juicing so nothing goes to waste. You can use the zest from any citrus fruit.

These sugar-coated strips are a beautiful garnish for ice cream, finished cakes, or fruit tarts. Or use it in recipes: drain the zest (skip the rolling-in-sugar step), chop it, and fold into ice cream, scone doughs, or cake batter. It works wonderfully to add a bit of citrus to any recipe.

## AT A GLANCE

WAITING AND COOLING TIME:
At least 2½ hours

SHELF LIFE: Nearly indefinitely when kept in syrup in the refrigerator; several weeks once rolled in sugar

3 navel oranges
1¼ cups granulated sugar
1½ cups water
About ½ cup turbinado sugar or other coarse sugar, for rolling

1. Use a vegetable peeler to remove the zest from the oranges, keeping the strips as wide as possible. Or use a channel knife (the type used by bartenders to make a "twist" for your martini) instead.

2. Fill two small nonreactive saucepans with water and bring to a boil over medium-high heat. When the first one comes to a boil, add the strips of zest all at once and stir to submerge them all. When the water comes back to a boil, drain the zest and repeat the process in the second pan. (This process reduces the amount of bitterness in the zest and helps soften it.)

3. In one of the empty saucepans, combine the granulated sugar and 1½ cups water and bring to a simmer over medium-high heat. Add the zest strips and stir to coat them evenly with the syrup. Partially cover the pan, reduce the heat to low, and cook gently until the zest is softened and appears translucent about ¼ inch in from the edge, about 1 hour.

4. Remove from the heat and let the zest cool in the syrup. If not using right away, transfer the zest and syrup to a container and refrigerate.

5. If you're using the zest as a garnish, set a wire rack over a rimmed baking sheet. Remove the zest strips from the syrup and arrange them on the rack. Let drain for 30 minutes or so, then cut into thin strips and roll in the turbinado. Allow the zest to dry on the rack for an hour or two before using. For longer storage, transfer to an airtight container and keep at room temperature.

> **MAKE IT YOUR OWN**
> * You can use almost any type of citrus in this recipe: lemon, grapefruit, orange, pomelo, sliced kumquats . . . the list goes on and on!

# LEMON GINGERSNAPS

Makes about 45 cookies | Pictured on page 151

These are some of our most popular cookies, both at the Creamery and the Market where they're also sold. They're more than your average gingersnap—they have classic ginger-and-molasses flavor but are brightened with lemon zest and a bit of lemon oil. A roll in turbinado sugar makes them extra sparkly and crunchy.

## AT A GLANCE

SPECIAL EQUIPMENT: Microplane
or other rasp grater

CHILLING TIME: At least
2 hours or up to overnight

SHELF LIFE:
1 week

4³/₄ cups (1 pound, 3 ounces) unbleached
all-purpose flour

2 tablespoons ground ginger

2 teaspoons ground cinnamon

2 teaspoons baking soda

1 teaspoon kosher salt

Finely grated zest of 2 large lemons

2 cups granulated sugar

1¹/₂ cups (12 ounces) unsalted butter, at room
temperature

¹/₂ cup dark molasses

2 large eggs

³/₄ teaspoon lemon oil (see Note, page 170)

About ³/₄ cup turbinado sugar, for rolling

1. In a medium bowl, whisk together the flour, ginger, cinnamon, baking soda, salt, and zest and set aside.

2. Put the granulated sugar and butter in the bowl of a stand mixer. Beat with the paddle attachment on medium-high speed until light in color and fluffy, about 2 minutes. Add the molasses and mix until blended. Scrape down the sides of the bowl. With the motor running, add the eggs one at a time. Mix until blended, about 30 seconds. Add the lemon oil and mix again.

3. Add the flour mixture and mix on low speed just until the dough comes together, about 30 seconds.

4. Cover the bowl with plastic wrap and chill until the dough is firm, at least 2 hours or up to overnight.

5. When you're ready to bake, position racks in the top and bottom thirds of the oven and preheat the oven to 350°F. Line two baking sheets with parchment paper or nonstick mats.

6. Scoop up 2 tablespoons of dough (we use a 1-ounce ice cream scoop) and form the dough into a ball. Repeat until all the dough

CONTINUED

has been shaped. Roll the balls in the turbinado sugar and place them 2½ inches apart on the baking sheets. Flatten the balls slightly with the palm of your hand so that they're about ½ inch thick.

7.  Bake for 6 minutes, and then rotate the baking sheets top to bottom and front to back. Continue to bake until the cookies have darkened slightly in color, look dry on the surface, and the edges are slightly firm to the touch, 5 to 7 minutes longer.

Let the cookies cool for a minute on the baking sheets, then transfer to a rack and let cool completely. Bake the remaining dough balls. Store the cookies in an airtight container.

**NOTE:** Lemon oil (see Sources, page 210) gives the cookies a boost of citrusy flavor. Find it in specialty grocery stores, baking supply shops, or online. You could make the cookies without it, but it does make them extra-lemony!

**SERVE IT WITH . . .**

❋ Pumpkin Pie Ice Cream (page 185), Brown Sugar Ice Cream with a Ginger-Caramel Swirl (page 63), or Ginger Ice Cream (page 178)

# LEMON CURD *or* SAUCE

Makes 1 1/3 cups curd or up to 2 2/3 cups sauce

This recipe is two recipes in one! It makes a thick, rich lemon curd that's great for scones and tarts. You can also thin it out with a little heavy cream for a mouth-puckering sauce that's perfect for ice cream sundaes.

It's important that your butter be at room temperature. If it's cold, it will lower the temperature of the curd and won't blend smoothly.

## AT A GLANCE

| SPECIAL EQUIPMENT: Microplane or other rasp grater | CHILLING TIME: 2 hours | SHELF LIFE: 2 weeks |
|---|---|---|

3 medium lemons (2 Meyer and 1 Eureka, or all Eureka)

7 large egg yolks

3/4 cup sugar

6 tablespoons (3 ounces) unsalted butter, cut into 1/2-inch pieces, at room temperature

1 cup heavy cream, plus more as needed, if making sauce

1. Put about 2 inches of water in the bottom of a double boiler or medium saucepan and bring to a simmer over medium-high heat. If you are using a gas stove, make sure the flames are not coming up around the pan; this will scorch your lemon curd very quickly.

2. Finely grate the zest from the lemons into the top of the double boiler or the non-reactive bowl you will be using to make your curd (you should have about 3 tablespoons) and set aside. Juice the lemons and measure out 1/2 cup juice (if using a mix of lemon types, make sure at least one-third of the juice is from Eureka lemons). Save the rest for another use.

3. Whisk the yolks into the zest, and then whisk in the sugar. Add the lemon juice and whisk to blend. Put the double boiler insert or bowl over but not touching the simmering water. Cook, whisking frequently, until the mixture is thick and puddinglike and leaves a trail when stirred, about 10 minutes. (Check the water level periodically and add more if it threatens to boil away.)

4. When the curd has thickened, remove from the heat and pour through a fine-mesh strainer into a bowl. (You will be straining out all of the grated zest, whose flavor is now infused in the curd itself. If you were to leave the zest in, the curd would have an odd mouthfeel.) Whisk in the butter a few pieces at a time until completely blended. Lay plastic wrap directly on the surface of the curd and refrigerate until completely chilled, about 2 hours.

   At this point you have a wonderful lemon curd, which you can use for a lemon tart or condiment for scones.

5. If you'd like to turn the lemon curd into a sauce, put about 1/2 cup of the curd in a bowl and slowly whisk in heavy cream, starting with 1 cup, to thin to your liking.

# HERBS *and* SPICES

**WHEN YOU APPROACH BI-RITE CREAMERY,** its signature sweet aroma announces its presence well before you catch a glimpse of the storefront. The warm combo of vanilla, sugar, cream, and butter permeates the air and always makes our shop smell delicious. But it's our recipes that use spices that really get the attention of passersby. It never fails. Whenever we are baking Evadne's Gingerbread (page 193) or anything else with dried spices, the heady scent wafts out onto the sidewalk and people poke their heads in the door to ask what's cooking. Those sweet spicy smells are hard to ignore—or resist!

For ice cream, we generally prefer to add herbs or spices to the hot cream and milk mixture, let them infuse until the desired flavor is achieved, then strain the mixture before incorporating the egg yolks. Doing it this way makes it possible to coax out the desired flavor with precision. We want a full, intense flavor, but we don't want to let the ingredients steep so long that they overextract and become bitter. The key to success is to taste the mixture periodically as it steeps. At first you will just taste cream, but you'll soon start to taste more and more of the herbs or spices in the cream mixture. Stop when you have an intense but not bitter flavor, remembering that the flavors will be muted somewhat once the ice cream is frozen. We give guidelines for the timing in each of the recipes that use this technique, but your taste buds are the best tool!

## BUYING AND USING SPICES

Finding organic spices, which are now readily available, should be your first priority when shopping. So many commercially grown spices are sprayed with the toxic chemical methyl iodide, and it's not like you can wash it off the spices before using them.

Buy spices in small quantities to ensure that you use them up before they go stale. Many natural food stores offer spices in bulk, allowing you to purchase as much or as little as you need. We get most of our spices from Spicely, a company committed to growing spices in a sustainable, environmentally friendly manner. We buy their products in bulk, but their spices packaged for retail sale are widely available and ideal for the home cook: they come in small quantities (about 2 tablespoons, depending on the spice) and are packaged in an ecologically mindful way.

You'll get much more flavor by buying whole spices and grinding them yourself as you need them. Almost any whole spice can easily be ground in a coffee grinder; nutmeg does best on a fine rasp grater. (Cinnamon and cloves are two spices we buy in ground form, as well as whole, because it's almost impossible to achieve a fine powder by grinding them yourself.)

Store spices in individual airtight containers away from heat and light. A drawer or cabinet is best; next to or above the stove is probably the worst place to keep them!

Try to use spices within six months to a year of purchase. Shelf life varies from one spice to the next, but your nose will tell you whether a spice has any punch left. If you take a whiff and can't immediately identify the spice by scent alone, toss it and refresh your supply. Whole spices have a much longer shelf life due to their minimal surface area exposed to oxygen—just one more reason to buy spices whole when you can.

We frequently toast spices in order to "bloom" their flavor and aroma. This simple process of heating the spices helps to activate and release the flavors.

## BUYING AND USING HERBS AND OTHER FRESH AROMATICS

Much of the information you just read about spices also applies to herbs and fresh aromatics like ginger. It's always best to buy organic herbs, but if they're not available, at least you have the option to wash herbs before using them. Either rinse them in cool water and pat dry, or gently wipe them off with a damp paper towel.

As with spices, we typically infuse fresh herbs into our ice cream base and then strain them out. Not only do herbs like basil and mint turn black when they come in contact with hot milk and cream, but they also have an unappetizing texture when frozen. Plus, they release their flavors very quickly and become bitter if oversteeped (even more so than spices), so we prefer to let the herbs' flavor release into the base and then get the herbs out of there!

# BASIL ICE CREAM

Makes about 1 quart

This is the perfect recipe to try when you're ready to venture a little off the beaten path. Most people think of basil, a cousin to mint, as a savory ingredient. However, its slight licorice flavor lends itself to sweet things, too. Make this recipe in the summer, when basil is extra fragrant and flavorful. You won't get the same results using basil grown in a hothouse in the middle of winter.

## AT A GLANCE

| TECHNIQUE: | SPECIAL EQUIPMENT: | INFUSING AND CHILLING TIME: | SHELF LIFE: |
|---|---|---|---|
| Ice cream (page 12) | Ice cream machine | 20 minutes, plus 2 hours or overnight | 1 week |

2 cups heavy cream

3/4 cup 1% or 2% milk

1/2 cup sugar

1/4 teaspoon kosher salt

15 to 20 fresh basil leaves, torn or chopped fine into 1/8-inch pieces

5 large egg yolks

### INFUSE THE MILK/CREAM

1. In a heavy nonreactive saucepan, stir together the cream, milk, half of the sugar (1/4 cup), and salt. Put the pan over medium-high heat.

2. When the mixture just begins to bubble around the edges, stir in the basil. When slight bubbling resumes around the edges of the pan, remove from the heat and cover the pan.

3. Let steep for about 20 minutes, or until the cream mixture has a distinct sweet basil flavor. (Taste it to monitor the progress; the mixture will become bitter if oversteeped.) Don't be alarmed if the basil turns black; it won't affect the flavor or color of the ice cream.

### MAKE THE BASE

4. In a medium heatproof bowl, whisk the yolks just to break them up, then whisk in the remaining sugar (1/4 cup). Set aside.

5. Uncover the cream mixture and put the pan over medium-high heat. When the mixture approaches a bare simmer, reduce the heat to medium.

6. Carefully scoop out about 1/2 cup of the hot cream mixture and, whisking the eggs constantly, add the cream to the bowl with the egg yolks. Repeat, adding another 1/2 cup of the hot cream to the bowl with the yolks. Using a heatproof rubber spatula, stir the cream in the saucepan as you slowly pour the egg-and-cream mixture from the bowl into the pan.

7. Cook the mixture carefully over medium heat, stirring constantly, until it is thickened, coats the back of a spatula, and holds a clear path when you run your finger across the spatula, 1 to 2 minutes longer.

8.  Strain the base through a fine-mesh strainer into a clean container. Set the container into an ice-water bath, wash your spatula, and use it to stir the base occasionally until it is cool. Remove the container from the ice-water bath, cover with plastic wrap, and refrigerate the base for at least 2 hours or overnight.

FREEZE THE ICE CREAM

9.  Freeze in your ice cream machine according to the manufacturer's instructions. While the ice cream is churning, put the container you'll use to store the ice cream into the freezer. Enjoy right away or, for a firmer ice cream, transfer to the chilled container and freeze for at least 4 hours.

### MAKE IT YOUR OWN

❊ Experiment with different varieties of basil or other leafy fresh herbs such as lemon verbena. Each herb will require a different infusion time, so be sure to taste along the way.

### SERVE IT WITH . . .

❊ Cheesecake Ice Cream (page 41)
❊ Sliced Strawberry Topping (page 149)
❊ Mandarin Orange Olive Oil Ice Cream (page 160)

# GINGER ICE CREAM

Makes about 1 quart

The first time Anne had ginger ice cream she fell in love with it. It was spicy and had just the right amount of hot and cold at the same time. Topped with hot fudge sauce, it's the perfect dessert. After experimenting with different recipes, we found that it really helps to blanch your ginger briefly before steeping it in the cream and milk. This reduces the amount of the enzyme in the ginger that can cause the dairy to curdle—but it still has plenty of flavor to infuse into the ice cream. Unlike most of our ice cream recipes, which call for 1 percent or 2 percent milk, this one uses whole milk. The additional fat offers extra insurance against curdling.

## AT A GLANCE

| TECHNIQUE: | SPECIAL EQUIPMENT: | INFUSING AND CHILLING TIME: | SHELF LIFE: |
|---|---|---|---|
| Ice cream (page 12) | Ice cream machine | 45 minutes, plus 2 hours or overnight | 1 week |

2¹/₂ ounces fresh ginger (a knob about 5¹/₂ inches long by 1 inch wide)

2 cups heavy cream

1 cup whole milk

¹/₂ cup sugar

¹/₄ teaspoon kosher salt

6 large egg yolks

2 tablespoons finely chopped candied ginger (optional)

### INFUSE THE MILK/CREAM

1. Peel the ginger and slice very thinly. Put the ginger in a nonreactive saucepan and add just enough water to cover. Put the pan over medium-high heat, bring to a boil, and boil for 1 minute. Remove from the heat, drain the ginger, and put it back in the pan. Stir in the cream, milk, half of the sugar (¹/₄ cup), and the salt.

2. Return the pan to medium-high heat. When the mixture just begins to bubble around the edges, remove from the heat and cover the pan. Let steep for 30 to 45 minutes, or until the cream mixture has an intense ginger flavor. (Taste it to monitor the progress; the mixture will be come bitter if oversteeped.)

### MAKE THE BASE

3. In a medium heatproof bowl, whisk the yolks just to break them up, then whisk in the remaining sugar (¹/₄ cup). Set aside.

4. Uncover the cream mixture and put the pan over medium-high heat. When the mixture approaches a bare simmer, reduce the heat to medium.

5. Carefully scoop out about ¹/₂ cup of the hot cream mixture and, whisking the eggs constantly, add the cream to the bowl with the

egg yolks. Repeat, adding another ½ cup of the hot cream to the bowl with the yolks. Using a heatproof rubber spatula, stir the cream in the saucepan as you slowly pour the egg-and-cream mixture from the bowl into the pan.

6. Cook the mixture carefully over medium heat, stirring constantly, until it is thickened, coats the back of a spatula, and holds a clear path when you run your finger across the spatula, 1 to 2 minutes longer.

7. Strain the base through a fine-mesh strainer into a clean container. Set the container into an ice-water bath, wash your spatula, and use it to stir the base occasionally until it is cool. Remove the container from the ice-water bath, cover with plastic wrap, and refrigerate the base for at least 2 hours or overnight.

## FREEZE THE ICE CREAM

8. Freeze in your ice cream machine according to the manufacturer's instructions. While the ice cream is churning, put the container you'll use to store the ice cream into the freezer. If using candied ginger, add it in the last minute or so of churning, or fold it in by hand after transferring the ice cream to the chilled container. Enjoy right away or, for a firmer ice cream, freeze for at least 4 hours.

**SERVE IT WITH . . .**
- ❊ Any sorbet or granita
- ❊ Hot Fudge Sauce (page 93)
- ❊ Blueberry-Lemon Sauce (page 150) and Lemon Gingersnaps (page 169) to make the sundae pictured on page 151

# HONEY LAVENDER ICE CREAM

Makes about 1 quart

There is no middle ground with this ice cream: people who try it either love it or hate it. Those who don't like it say it tastes like soap. To us (and its many fans), it may smell like soap, but the flavor—a distinct lavender flavor against a honey backdrop—is a real treat. This remains one of the most popular flavors among our staff.

We get our honey from Bobby Winston, a beekeeper in Sonoma County, California, who harvests his hives exclusively for us. We get 80 gallons of honey from him every year, which come to us all at once in 5-gallon buckets. It's a wildflower blend, relatively dark and stronger in flavor than your average clover honey, with a slight molasses note. It results in a pronounced honey flavor in the finished ice cream, but you can use a lighter flavored honey for a more delicate effect.

## AT A GLANCE

| TECHNIQUE: | SPECIAL EQUIPMENT: | INFUSING AND CHILLING TIME: | SHELF LIFE: |
|---|---|---|---|
| Ice cream (page 12) | Ice cream machine | 20 minutes, plus 2 hours or overnight | 1 week |

1³/₄ cups heavy cream

³/₄ cup 1% or 2% milk

¹/₂ cup honey

¹/₄ teaspoon kosher salt

2 tablespoons organic dried lavender

5 large egg yolks

### INFUSE THE MILK/CREAM

1. In a heavy nonreactive saucepan, stir together the cream, milk, honey, and salt.

2. Put the pan over medium-high heat. When the mixture just begins to bubble around the edges, remove from the heat and whisk in the lavender. Cover the pan and let steep for 15 to 20 minutes, or until the cream has taken on a distinct lavender flavor. (Stir it occasionally and taste it to monitor the progress.)

3. Strain through a fine-mesh strainer into a bowl, being sure to press on the lavender to extract all of the cream mixture. Rinse out the saucepan and return the infused cream to the pan.

## MAKE THE BASE

4. In a medium heatproof bowl, whisk the yolks just to break them up and set aside.

5. Put the pan of cream and milk over medium-high heat. When the mixture approaches a bare simmer, reduce the heat to medium.

6. Carefully scoop out about ½ cup of the hot cream mixture and, whisking the eggs constantly, add the cream to the bowl with the egg yolks. Repeat, adding another ½ cup of the hot cream to the bowl with the yolks. Using a heatproof rubber spatula, stir the cream in the saucepan as you slowly pour the egg-and-cream mixture from the bowl into the pan.

7. Cook the mixture carefully over medium heat, stirring constantly, until it is thickened, coats the back of a spatula, and holds a clear path when you run your finger across the spatula, 1 to 2 minutes longer.

8. Strain the base through a fine-mesh strainer into a clean container. Set the container into an ice-water bath, wash your spatula, and use it to stir the base occasionally until it is cool. Remove the container from the ice-water bath, cover with plastic wrap, and refrigerate the base for at least 2 hours or overnight.

## FREEZE THE ICE CREAM

9. Freeze in your ice cream machine according to the manufacturer's instructions. While the ice cream is churning, put the container you'll use to store the ice cream into the freezer. Enjoy right away or, for a firmer ice cream, transfer to the chilled container and freeze for at least 4 hours.

### MAKE IT YOUR OWN

❋ Try fresh rosemary in place of the lavender. The steeping time may vary (and too much rosemary can be an overwhelming flavor), so be sure to taste along the way.

### SERVE IT WITH . . .

❋ Balsamic Strawberry Ice Cream (page 138)

❋ Vanilla Ice Cream (page 35), Hot Fudge Sauce (page 93), and Whipped Cream (page 51) for a combo called Best Friends Sundae by Anne's daughter Zoe and her best friend Hannah, so named because it contains each of their favorite flavors!

❋ Hot Fudge Sauce (page 93), blood orange olive oil, and a sprinkle of Maldon sea salt (a combination developed by one of our scoopers, Josh, who named it The Dainty Gentleman)

# MINT CHIP ICE CREAM

Makes about 1 quart | Pictured on page 76

This is the favorite flavor of Anne's husband, Sam, who also happens to be the man behind Bi-Rite Market. It's also one of the most popular flavors among our younger guests. We make our own chocolate chips using melted bittersweet chocolate with a tiny bit of canola oil added to it. The oil gives the chocolate a lower melting point, so the chips soften and melt in your mouth. To make the chips, we spread the melted chocolate mixture very thinly on baking sheets, freeze it, then break the hardened chocolate into small pieces. This creates thin shards that have an irresistable texture in the finished ice cream. If time is of the essence, you can use very finely chopped chocolate instead, but we feel that making our own chips gives the ice cream a really nice consistency and is definitely worth the extra step.

## AT A GLANCE

| TECHNIQUE: | SPECIAL EQUIPMENT: | CHILLING TIME: | SHELF LIFE: |
|---|---|---|---|
| Ice cream (page 12) | Ice cream machine and offset spatula | 2 hours or overnight | 1 week |

5 large egg yolks

1/2 cup sugar

2 cups heavy cream

1 cup 1% or 2% milk

1/4 teaspoon kosher salt

### CHOCOLATE CHIPS

4 ounces bittersweet chocolate (52% to 60% cacao), finely chopped (3/4 cup)

2 teaspoons canola oil

1 teaspoon organic peppermint extract

### MAKE THE BASE

1. In a medium heatproof bowl, whisk the yolks just to break them up, then whisk in half of the sugar (1/4 cup). Set aside.

2. In a heavy nonreactive saucepan, stir together the cream, milk, salt, and the remaining sugar (1/4 cup) and put the pan over medium-high heat. When the mixture approaches a bare simmer, reduce the heat to medium.

3. Carefully scoop out about 1/2 cup of the hot cream mixture and, whisking the eggs constantly, add the cream to the bowl with the egg yolks. Repeat, adding another 1/2 cup of the hot cream to the bowl with the yolks. Using a heatproof rubber spatula, stir the cream in the saucepan as you slowly pour the egg-and-cream mixture from the bowl into the pan.

4. Cook the mixture carefully over medium heat, stirring constantly, until it is thickened, coats the back of a spatula, and holds a clear path when you run your finger across the spatula, 1 to 2 minutes longer.

5. Strain the base through a fine-mesh strainer into a clean container. Set the container into an ice-water bath, wash your spatula, and use it to stir the base occasionally until it is cool. Remove the container from the ice-water bath, cover with plastic wrap, and refrigerate the base for at least 2 hours or overnight.

## WHILE THE BASE IS CHILLING, MAKE THE CHIPS

6. Line a rimmed baking sheet with parchment paper and set aside.

7. Put ½ inch of water in the bottom of a double boiler or medium saucepan and bring to a simmer over medium-high heat. If you are using a gas stove, make sure the flames are not coming up around the pan, which can cause the chocolate to scorch.

   Put the chopped chocolate in the top of the double boiler or a medium heat-proof bowl. Put the pan or bowl over but not touching the simmering water. Stir frequently until the chocolate is melted and completely smooth, 2 to 4 minutes. Remove from the heat and stir in the canola oil.

8. Pour the chocolate onto the prepared baking sheet and use an offset spatula to spread it into a thin, even layer. Refrigerate or freeze until hardened and brittle (30 minutes in the refrigerator, 20 minutes in the freezer).

9. When the chocolate is completely set, remove it from the refrigerator or freezer and peel it off of the parchment paper. Working quickly, break the chocolate into small pieces and put them in a bowl. (If you work too slowly, the thin chocolate will start to melt in your hands. If this happens, just return everything to the refrigerator or freezer for a few minutes to reharden.) Put the chocolate chips in the freezer until you are ready to add them to the churned ice cream.

## FREEZE THE ICE CREAM

10. Whisk the peppermint extract into the chilled base.

11. Freeze in your ice cream machine according to the manufacturer's instructions. While the ice cream is churning, put the container you'll use to store the ice cream into the freezer. Add the frozen chocolate chips in the last minute or so of churning, or fold them in by hand after transferring the ice cream to the chilled container. Enjoy right away or, for a firmer ice cream, freeze for at least 4 hours.

---

**MAKE IT YOUR OWN**
* Substitute finely chopped candy canes for the chocolate chips for a Christmassy delight! Sprinkle on additional chopped candy canes as a topping.

**SERVE IT WITH . . .**
* Cookies and Cream Ice Cream (page 84) for a kid's dream sundae!

---

# PEPPERMINT EXTRACT

You may be surprised to see that we rely on peppermint extract for our Mint Chip Ice Cream. Practicality is the reason—it takes a lot of fresh mint to get the intensity of flavor we're looking for, and so we use pure peppermint extract made from the plant's essential oils. You could, of course, infuse your base with fresh mint using the technique in the Basil Ice Cream (page 176), perhaps supplementing with a drop or two of peppermint extract as needed.

# PEACH LEAF ICE CREAM

Makes about 1 quart

This recipe was inspired by the recipe for peach leaf parfait in the *Chez Panisse Fruit* cookbook. When you steep peach leaves in milk and cream, they impart a wonderful bitter almond flavor that is truly special. If you are lucky enough to have a peach tree in your backyard (or access to one), it's best to pick young, tender leaves. You may also be able to find peach leaves by asking for them at your local farmers' market.

## AT A GLANCE

| TECHNIQUE: | SPECIAL EQUIPMENT: | CHILLING TIME: | SHELF LIFE: |
|---|---|---|---|
| Ice cream (page 12) | Ice cream machine | 2 hours or overnight | 1 week |

1³/4 cups heavy cream

³/4 cup 1% or 2% milk

1/2 cup sugar

1/4 teaspoon kosher salt

10 to 12 fresh peach leaves (unsprayed or organic), rinsed and patted dry

5 large egg yolks

### INFUSE THE MILK/CREAM

1. In a heavy nonreactive saucepan, stir together the cream, milk, half of the sugar (1/4 cup), and the salt.

2. Put the pan over medium-high heat. Crush the leaves gently in your hands to release their flavor and add them to the pan. When the mixture just begins to bubble around the edges, remove from the heat and cover the pan. Let steep for 15 to 20 minutes, or until a mellow bitter almond flavor has infused into the cream mixture. (Taste it to monitor the progress; the mixture will become bitter if oversteeped.)

### MAKE THE BASE

3. In a medium heatproof bowl, whisk the yolks just to break them up, then whisk in the remaining sugar (1/4 cup). Set aside.

4. Uncover the cream mixture and put the pan over medium-high heat. When the mixture approaches a bare simmer, reduce the heat to medium.

5. Carefully scoop out about 1/2 cup of the hot cream mixture and, whisking the eggs constantly, add the cream to the bowl with the egg yolks. Repeat, adding another 1/2 cup of the hot cream to the bowl with the yolks. Using a heatproof rubber spatula, stir the cream in the saucepan as you slowly pour the egg-and-cream mixture from the bowl into the pan.

6. Cook the mixture carefully over medium heat, stirring constantly, until it is thickened, coats the back of a spatula, and holds a clear path when you run your finger across the spatula, 1 to 2 minutes longer.

7. Strain the base through a fine-mesh strainer into a clean container. Set the container into an ice-water bath, wash your spatula, and use it to stir the base occasionally until it is cool.

Remove the container from the ice-water bath, cover with plastic wrap, and refrigerate the base for at least 2 hours or overnight.

**FREEZE THE ICE CREAM**

8. Freeze in your ice cream machine according to the manufacturer's instructions. While the ice cream is churning, put the container you'll use to store the ice cream into the freezer. Enjoy right away or, for a firmer ice cream, transfer to the chilled container and freeze for at least 4 hours.

> **SERVE IT WITH . . .**
> ❋ Peach compote or fresh berries

# PUMPKIN PIE ICE CREAM

Makes about 1 quart | Pictured on page 194

This is one of our most popular holiday flavors. Every October our guests start clamoring for our pumpkin ice cream, so we put it into regular rotation around that time and keep making it through the holidays. As soon as Christmas is over, though, people begin to lose interest in it! They may ask for Balsamic Strawberry Ice Cream (page 138) all year round, but nobody wants pumpkin ice cream after New Year's.

During that autumnal period when our guests *are* excited about this flavor, we make a seasonal sundae with this ice cream, Evadne's Gingerbread (page 193), warm Caramel Sauce (page 71), Spiced Pecans (page 132), and Whipped Cream (page 51). The ice cream is lovely on its own as a simple finish to a holiday meal, but it's even better with gingerbread in an ice cream cake, or with a gingersnap crust as an ice cream pie.

**AT A GLANCE** ・・・・・・・・・・・・・・・・・・・・・・・・・・・・・・・・・・・・・・・・・・・・・・・・・・・・・・・・・・・・・・・・・・・・・・・・・・・・

| TECHNIQUE: | SPECIAL EQUIPMENT: | CHILLING TIME: | SHELF LIFE |
|---|---|---|---|
| Ice cream (page 12) | Ice cream machine | 2 hours or overnight | 1 week |

6 large egg yolks

1/2 teaspoon ground cinnamon

1/2 teaspoon ground ginger

3/4 cup packed light or dark brown sugar

2 cups heavy cream

1/2 cup 1% or 2% milk

1/2 teaspoon kosher salt

3/4 cup pumpkin purée (see Note, page 186)

1/2 teaspoon pure vanilla extract

**MAKE THE BASE**

1. In a medium heatproof bowl, whisk the yolks just to break them up, then whisk in the cinnamon, ginger, and half of the brown sugar (6 tablespoons). Set aside.

2. In a heavy nonreactive saucepan, stir together the cream, milk, salt, and the remaining sugar (6 tablespoons) and put

CONTINUED

the pan over medium-high heat. When the mixture approaches a bare simmer, reduce the heat to medium.

3. Carefully scoop out about ½ cup of the hot cream mixture and, whisking the eggs constantly, add the cream to the bowl with the egg yolks. Repeat, adding another ½ cup of the hot cream to the bowl with the yolks. Using a heatproof rubber spatula, stir the cream in the saucepan as you slowly pour the egg-and-cream mixture from the bowl into the pan.

4. Cook the mixture carefully over medium heat, stirring constantly, until it is thickened, coats the back of a spatula, and holds a clear path when you run your finger across the spatula, 1 to 2 minutes longer.

5. Strain the base through a fine-mesh strainer into a clean container. Set the container into an ice-water bath, wash your spatula, and use it to stir the base occasionally until it is cool. Remove the container from the ice-water bath, cover with plastic wrap, and refrigerate the base for at least 2 hours or overnight.

### FREEZE THE ICE CREAM

6. Whisk the vanilla into the chilled base.

7. Freeze in your ice cream machine according to the manufacturer's instructions. While the ice cream is churning, put the container you'll use to store the ice cream into the freezer. Enjoy right away or, for a firmer ice cream, transfer to the chilled container and freeze for at least 4 hours.

> **NOTE:** You can use canned or homemade cooked puréed pumpkin for this recipe. If you make your own purée, roast the pumpkin in the oven first to help concentrate the flavor and reduce the water content. If you use canned, be sure you get the plain variety; those labeled "pumpkin pie mix" contain sugar and spices and will throw off the recipe here.

# EGG NOG ICE CREAM

Makes about 1 quart

When you think about it, egg nog is not so different from ice cream base: they both contain egg yolks, cream, and sugar, and they both benefit from a spike of booze. Our version is enriched with extra egg yolks, nutmeg, cinnamon, and just the right amount of brandy (or rum). Be sure to grate your nutmeg just before using it. You'll get a lot more flavor that way.

Every year we tweak this recipe a little bit by changing the ratio of spices or using a different kind of spirit. Last year's version (shared here) was the best yet. It really does taste like egg nog and has a lovely soft consistency thanks to that bit of alcohol.

### AT A GLANCE

| TECHNIQUE: | SPECIAL EQUIPMENT: | CHILLING TIME: | SHELF LIFE: |
|---|---|---|---|
| Ice cream (page 12) | Ice cream machine | 2 hours or overnight | 1 week |

7 large egg yolks

1/2 cup sugar

2 cups heavy cream

3/4 cup 1% or 2% milk

1/2 teaspoon freshly grated nutmeg

1/4 teaspoon ground cinnamon

1/4 teaspoon kosher salt

2 tablespoons brandy or rum

1 teaspoon pure vanilla extract

## MAKE THE BASE

1. In a medium heatproof bowl, whisk the yolks just to break them up, then whisk in half of the sugar (1/4 cup). Set aside.

2. In a heavy nonreactive saucepan, whisk together the cream, milk, nutmeg, cinnamon, salt, and the remaining sugar (1/4 cup) and put the pan over medium-high heat. When the mixture approaches a bare simmer, reduce the heat to medium.

3. Carefully scoop out about 1/2 cup of the hot cream mixture and, whisking the eggs constantly, add the cream to the bowl with the egg yolks. Repeat, adding another 1/2 cup of the hot cream to the bowl with the yolks. Using a heatproof rubber spatula, stir the cream in the saucepan as you slowly pour the egg-and-cream mixture from the bowl into the pan.

4. Cook the mixture carefully over medium heat, stirring constantly, until it is thickened, coats the back of a spatula, and holds a clear path when you run your finger across the spatula, 1 to 2 minutes longer.

5. Strain the base through a fine-mesh strainer into a clean container. Set the container into an ice-water bath, wash your spatula, and use it to stir the base occasionally until it is cool. Remove the container from the ice-water bath, cover with plastic wrap, and refrigerate the base for at least 2 hours or up to overnight.

## FREEZE THE ICE CREAM

6. Whisk the brandy and vanilla into the base.

7. Freeze in your ice cream machine according to the manufacturer's instructions. While the ice cream is churning, put the container you'll use to store the ice cream into the freezer. Enjoy right away or, for a firmer ice cream, transfer to the chilled container and freeze for at least 4 hours.

---

**MAKE IT YOUR OWN**

❋ Try your favorite spirit instead of rum or brandy. Bourbon would be equally delicious!

**SERVE IT WITH . . .**

❋ Pumpkin Pie Ice Cream (page 185), Ricanelas Ice Cream (page 188), or Crème Fraîche Ice Cream (page 38)

❋ Vanilla Butterscotch Sauce (page 48)

❋ Brown Sugar Graham Crackers (page 66) to make an ice cream sandwich

# RICANELAS ICE CREAM

Makes about 1 quart

Our ice cream maker Ezequiel came up with this flavor, which is inspired by a popular cinnamon cookie made in his hometown in Mexico. Reinvented as an ice cream, the cookie becomes a cinnamon-infused ice cream with chopped Snickerdoodles (page 195) folded in. It's one of our most popular flavors with both our guests and our staff. The only problem people seem to have with it is trying to pronounce the name! (It's *ree-cah-NELL-ahs*.)

AT A GLANCE ••••••••••••••••••••••••••••••••••••••••••••••••••••••••••••••

| TECHNIQUE: | SPECIAL EQUIPMENT: | CHILLING TIME: | SHELF LIFE: |
|---|---|---|---|
| Ice cream (page 12) | Ice cream machine | 2 hours or overnight | 1 week |

5 large egg yolks

1/2 cup sugar

2 cups heavy cream

1 cup 1% or 2% milk

1 teaspoon ground cinnamon

1/4 teaspoon kosher salt

1 teaspoon pure vanilla extract

1 cup chopped Snickerdoodles (page 195), from 2 to 3 large cookies

## MAKE THE BASE

1. In a medium heatproof bowl, whisk the yolks just to break them up, then whisk in half of the sugar (1/4 cup). Set aside.

2. In a heavy nonreactive saucepan, whisk together the cream, milk, cinnamon, salt, and the remaining sugar (1/4 cup) and put the pan over medium-high heat. When the mixture approaches a bare simmer, reduce the heat to medium.

3. Carefully scoop out about 1/2 cup of the hot cream mixture and, whisking the eggs constantly, add the cream to the bowl with the egg yolks. Repeat, adding another 1/2 cup of the hot cream to the bowl with the yolks. Using a heatproof rubber spatula, stir the cream in the saucepan as you slowly pour the egg-and-cream mixture from the bowl into the pan.

4. Cook the mixture carefully over medium heat, stirring constantly, until it is thickened, coats the back of a spatula, and holds a clear path when you run your finger across the spatula, 1 to 2 minutes longer. (Don't worry if the cinnamon still looks a little clumpy.)

5. Strain the base through a fine-mesh strainer into a clean container. Set the container into an ice-water bath, wash your spatula, and use it to stir the base occasionally until it is cool. Remove the container from the ice-water bath, cover with plastic wrap, and refrigerate the base for at least 2 hours or overnight.

FREEZE THE ICE CREAM

6. Whisk the vanilla into the chilled base.

7. Freeze in your ice cream machine according to the manufacturer's instructions. While the ice cream is churning, put the container you'll use to store the ice cream into the freezer. Add the chopped cookies in the last minute or so of churning, or fold them in by hand after transferring the ice cream to the chilled container. Enjoy right away or, for a firmer ice cream, freeze for at least 4 hours.

> **MAKE IT YOUR OWN**
> ❋ For pure cinnamon flavor and smooth creamy texture, omit the Snickerdoodles.
>
> **SERVE IT WITH . . .**
> ❋ Brown Sugar Ice Cream with a Ginger-Caramel Swirl (page 63)—the original version of Kris's combo sundae (see page 64)
> ❋ Coffee Toffee Ice Cream (see Coffee Ice Cream, page 103) or Caramelized Banana Ice Cream (page 202)

# APPLE PIE ICE CREAM

Makes about 1 quart

Our kitchen manager, Debby, came up with this ice cream. She's big on inclusions (cookies and candies and other treats that are added to ice cream), and so she favors flavors that have lots of "stuff" in them. This re-creation of apple pie features cooked apples, brown sugar, and cinnamon, and a "crust" of cookies folded in at the end.

## AT A GLANCE

| TECHNIQUE: | SPECIAL EQUIPMENT: | CHILLING TIME: | SHELF LIFE: |
|---|---|---|---|
| Ice cream (page 12) | Ice cream machine | 2 hours or overnight | 1 week |

### FOR THE APPLES

1/4 cup packed light or dark brown sugar

1 tablespoon unsalted butter

2 medium apples (pippin, Granny Smith, or other firm, tart cooking apple), peeled, cored, and cut into 1-inch chunks

1 teaspoon ground cinnamon

### FOR THE BASE

5 large egg yolks

1/3 cup sugar

1 3/4 cups heavy cream

3/4 cup 1% or 2% milk

1/4 teaspoon kosher salt

1 teaspoon pure vanilla extract

1/2 cup chopped Snickerdoodles (page 195) or sugar cookies (in pieces about 1/4 inch)

## COOK THE APPLES

1. Combine the brown sugar and butter in a medium skillet and put the pan over medium heat. When the butter is melted and bubbly, add the apples and cinnamon. Cook, stirring frequently, until the apples are softened and most of the liquid has evaporated, 10 to 15 minutes. Remove from the heat and let cool.

## MAKE THE BASE

2. In a medium heatproof bowl, whisk the yolks just to break them up, then whisk in half of the sugar (about 2 1/2 tablespoons). Set aside.

3. In a heavy nonreactive saucepan, stir together the cream, milk, salt, and the remaining sugar and put the pan over medium-high heat. When the mixture approaches a bare simmer, reduce the heat to medium.

4. Carefully scoop out about ½ cup of the hot cream mixture and, whisking the eggs constantly, add the cream to the bowl with the egg yolks. Repeat, adding another ½ cup of the hot cream to the bowl with the yolks. Using a heatproof rubber spatula, stir the cream in the saucepan as you slowly pour the egg-and-cream mixture from the bowl into the pan.

5. Cook the mixture carefully over medium heat, stirring constantly, until it is thickened, coats the back of a spatula, and holds a clear path when you run your finger across the spatula, 1 to 2 minutes longer.

6. Strain the base through a fine-mesh strainer into a clean container. Set the container into an ice-water bath, wash your spatula, and use it to stir the base occasionally until it is cool. Remove the container from the ice-water bath, cover with plastic wrap, and refrigerate the base for at least 2 hours or overnight.

FREEZE THE ICE CREAM

7. Combine the purée with the vanilla and half of the chilled base in a blender or food processor. Purée until smooth.

8. Combine the puréed mixture and the remaining base and freeze in your ice cream machine according to the manufacturer's instructions. While the ice cream is churning, put the container you'll use to store the ice cream into the freezer. Add the chopped cookies in the last minute or so of churning, or fold them in by hand after transferring the ice cream to the chilled container. Enjoy right away or, for a firmer ice cream, freeze for at least 4 hours.

> **SERVE IT WITH . . .**
> ❋ Pumpkin Pie Ice Cream (page 185), Brown Sugar Ice Cream with a Ginger-Caramel Swirl (page 63), or Salted Caramel Ice Cream (page 61)
> ❋ A drizzle of Caramel Sauce (page 71)

# PICANTE GALIA MELON ICE POPS

Makes eight 3-ounce ice pops

Kris says, "I always look forward to this refreshing, summery pop. It reminds me of vacations in Mexico, where I've been served pieces of melon or mango sprinkled with lime, salt, and cayenne pepper. At the beach and with a nice cold beer in hand, I could eat that spicy fruit all day long!"

## AT A GLANCE

| TECHNIQUE: | SPECIAL EQUIPMENT: | CHILLING TIME: | SHELF LIFE: |
|---|---|---|---|
| Ice pops (page 20) | Ice pop molds | At least 4 hours | 1 week |

1 small Galia melon (about 2¹/₄ pounds), peeled, seeded and cut into chunks

¹/₂ cup 1:1 Simple Syrup (page 18), cooled

2 tablespoons fresh strained lime juice

¹/₄ teaspoon kosher salt

¹/₈ teaspoon cayenne pepper

MAKE THE BASE

1. In a food processor or blender, purée the melon until smooth. Strain through a fine-mesh strainer into a medium bowl. Add 6 tablespoons of the simple syrup, the lime juice, salt, and cayenne.

2. Taste the base. It should taste just a bit too sweet (once frozen, it will lose some of its sweetness). Add the remaining simple syrup if you need it.

FREEZE THE ICE POPS

3. Transfer the base to a liquid measuring cup and pour into the ice pop molds. Insert the sticks and freeze until completely solid, about 4 hours. Unmold just before serving.

> **MAKE IT YOUR OWN**
> ❋ We like to use Galia melon, which looks like a cross between a cantaloupe and a honeydew. However, you could use almost any variety of melon in its place.

# EVADNE'S GINGERBREAD

Makes two 8-inch cakes (enough for two ice cream cakes) or about 16 cupcakes | Pictured on page 194

Anne says, "This recipe came to me from my dear friend and co-worker Shannan Hobbs. She got it from her Great Granny Tatum, who was a housewife in the 1920s. In those days, apparently it was common for authors to sprinkle recipes throughout novels that were targeted to women, thus ensuring that a housewife's time was always well spent. Great Granny Tatum discovered this recipe in a novel in which the main character, named Evadne, goes to the kitchen and whips up gingerbread. The recipe has been in Shannan's family ever since."

This simple, versatile cake can be layered with lemon curd and buttercream as a layer cake or made into cupcakes and topped with cream cheese frosting. During the holidays, we use this gingerbread as the bottom layer in our pumpkin ice cream cake.

## AT A GLANCE

| | | |
|---|---|---|
| SPECIAL EQUIPMENT: Two round cake pans, 8 inches in diameter and 3 inches deep, or two standard muffin pans | COOLING TIME:<br>1 to 2 hours | SHELF LIFE:<br>5 days |

Nonstick cooking spray or unsalted butter, for the cake pan

2 cups (9 ounces) unbleached all-purpose flour

2 teaspoons baking soda

1 teaspoon ground cloves

1 teaspoon ground ginger

1 teaspoon ground cinnamon

1 teaspoon kosher salt

1 cup canola or other neutral-flavored oil

3/4 cup plus 2 tablespoons sugar

1/2 cup dark molasses

3 large eggs

1 cup boiling water

1. If making cakes, position a rack in the center of the oven; if making cupcakes, position racks in the upper third and lower third of the oven. Preheat the oven to 350°F. If making cakes, spray or butter two round cake pans, each 8 inches in diamter and 3 inches deep, and line the bottoms with parchment paper. If making cupcakes, line sixteen cups of two standard muffin tins with paper or foil liners.

2. In a medium bowl, whisk together the flour, baking soda, cloves, ginger, cinnamon, and salt and set aside.

3. In the bowl of a stand mixer with the paddle attachment, combine the oil, sugar, and molasses. Mix on medium speed until blended, 15 seconds. With the motor running, add the eggs one at a time, completely mixing in each egg before adding the next.

CONTINUED

Ice cream cake with Evadne's Gingerbread, Pumpkin Pie Ice Cream (page 185), and Caramel Sauce (page 71)

Scrape down the sides of the bowl, add the flour mixture, and mix on low speed just until combined, about 30 seconds. Add the boiling water and mix on low speed just until blended.

4. Divide the batter between the cake pans or among the muffin cups (each cup should be about three-quarters full). Bake until the cakes spring back to a light touch and a toothpick inserted into the center comes out clean, 25 to 30 minutes for the cakes and 15 to 20 minutes for cupcakes.

5. Let the cakes cool in the pans for 45 minutes, then invert onto a wire rack. Remove the parchment and let cool completely. Let the cupcakes cool in the pans for 30 minutes before transferring to a wire rack, then let cool completely.

**NOTE:** A stand mixer isn't essential to the success of this recipe; you can also mix it by hand, which is probably how Great Granny Tatum did it!

**SERVE IT WITH . . .**

❊ Lemon Curd Sauce (page 171) and Whipped Cream (page 51)
❊ Meyer Lemon Ice Cream (page 156), Ginger Ice Cream (page 178), Ricanelas Ice Cream (page 188), or Honey Lavender Ice Cream (page 180)

# SNICKERDOODLES

Makes about 30 cookies

Snickerdoodles, for the uninitiated, are basically sugar cookies that get a dusting of cinnamon-sugar before baking. If you're making these to use them in Ricanelas Ice Cream (page 188), try baking them just a bit darker than you normally would. This helps ensure they stay crunchy once mixed into the ice cream.

## AT A GLANCE

**CHILLING AND COOLING TIME:** At least
2 hours or up to overnight

**SHELF LIFE:**
5 days

2 cups (9 ounces) unbleached all-purpose flour

2 teaspoons cream of tartar

1 teaspoon baking soda

$^1/_2$ teaspoon kosher salt

1 cup (8 ounces) unsalted butter, at room temperature

$1^1/_2$ cups sugar

2 large eggs

**FOR ROLLING**

1 tablespoon ground cinnamon

$^1/_4$ cup sugar

1. In a medium bowl, whisk together the flour, cream of tartar, baking soda, and salt and set aside.

2. In the bowl of a stand mixer with the paddle attachment, combine the butter and $1^1/_2$ cups sugar. Mix on medium-high speed until lightened in color and fluffy, about 2 minutes. Scrape down the bowl. With the motor running, add the eggs one at a time, completely mixing in each egg in before adding the next.

   Scrape down the sides of the bowl, add the flour mixture, and mix on low speed just until the dough comes together, about 30 seconds.

3. Cover the bowl with plastic wrap and chill until the dough is firm, at least 2 hours or up to overnight.

4. When you're ready to bake, position racks in the top and bottom thirds of the oven and preheat the oven to 350°F. Line two baking sheets with parchment paper or nonstick mats. In a small bowl, mix the cinnamon and ¼ cup of sugar.

   Scoop up 2 tablespoons of dough (we use a 1-ounce ice cream scoop) and form the dough into a ball. Repeat until all the dough has been shaped. Toss the dough balls in the cinnamon-sugar mixture and space them at least 3 inches apart on the baking sheets (they spread a lot during baking).

5. Bake for 5 minutes, then rotate the baking sheets top to bottom and front to back. Continue to bake until the cookies are golden brown on the edges, 7 to 9 minutes longer. (If you plan to use a few in the Ricanelas Ice Cream on page 188, bake them until golden brown in the center, 2 minutes extra.)

   Let cool for 5 minutes on the baking sheets, then transfer to a cooling rack. Bake the remaining dough balls. Let cool completely. Store in an airtight container.

# TROPICAL FRUITS

WE MAKE EVERY EFFORT to use local and seasonal fruits in our ice creams and treats, but we do make a few exceptions for tropical fruits that simply won't grow in Northern California. (Don't let all the palm trees that we have in San Francisco fool you!) How could we call ourselves an ice cream shop if we didn't offer banana splits? We also make an exception for mangoes, which are delectable on their own but become even more luscious and amazing as a sorbet. Even though these fruits don't grow nearby, we do everything we can to source organically grown fruit from producers who are taking care of their land.

## COCONUTS

For convenience, we use dried organic coconut and canned organic coconut milk in our bakery recipes. Little is lost in the path from whole coconut to these shelf-stable forms; they still provide great coconut flavor, and they're a lot easier to deal with than fresh coconut.

For ice creams and baked goods, we use dried shredded coconut (in fine wisps measuring $\frac{1}{16}$ inch to $\frac{1}{8}$ inch) in sweetened and/or unsweetened forms, depending on the desired effect. The one exception is our granola recipe on page 133, which uses flaked dried coconut (about $\frac{1}{4}$ inch wide) for extra crunch.

**Unsweetened dried coconut** provides pure coconut flavor and gives us more control over how much sugar we're adding to the mix; we use it anytime we want to infuse a liquid, such as when we're making our coconut ice cream base, or when it's the main ingredient, as in our macaroons. Most natural foods stores carry unsweetened dried coconut.

We use **sweetened dried coconut** for "finishing" items, like sprinkling over a cake or mixing into churned ice cream. The sugar gives the coconut a more pleasant texture and mouthfeel.

We always toast our coconut before using it to intensify and enhance its flavor. You can do this on the stove top (more energy efficient) or in the oven (more foolproof).

- **Oven method.** Position a rack in the center of the oven and preheat the oven to 350°F. Spread the coconut on a rimmed baking sheet and bake, stirring every 2 minutes, until golden brown, 4 to 6 minutes total.

- **Stove top method.** Put the coconut in a dry skillet and put the pan over medium heat. Stir constantly to prevent burning and toast until golden brown, about 4 minutes.

We use canned coconut milk in a few recipes, most notably in our Chocolate Coconut "Ice Cream" (page 204). Use organic if you can find it, but whatever you do, don't use "lite" because the reduced fat will produce disappointing results.

## PINEAPPLES

One great thing about pineapples is that they continue to ripen after picking, so even if you can only find green ones at the grocery store, it will eventually reach ripe perfection at home. Leave it on your counter to ripen (at the creamery we just leave them in their crates, stacked up in our hallway!). Pay attention to the pineapple in the days that follow: it will turn more golden or yellow as it ripens, and it will start to have a bit of "give" when you squeeze it (too much give means it's overripe). The true test is to smell the base. When it has a heady, floral aroma, it's ready to use.

**To trim and dice a pineapple,** first grab the leafy top and twist it until it comes off. (You can compost the top, or plant it in the ground to grow your own pineapple plant.) Slice about ½ inch off of the top and bottom of the fruit to expose the flesh and create a more stable base. Set the pineapple on one of the cut ends and slice down to remove a strip of rind, following the natural curvature of the fruit. Repeat all the way around. If you're making ice pops or sorbet, don't worry if some of the "eyes" remain in the fruit (they'll get strained out anyway), but if you're serving the fruit as is, you can use a paring knife to remove the eyes. Then, quarter the fruit lengthwise and trim the fibrous core from the center of each wedge. Compost or discard the rinds and core. Halve each wedge lengthwise, and then cut crosswise into chunks.

## MANGOES

Mangoes comes in many different sizes, shapes, flavors, and textures. Our favorite is the Manila (also called champagne or Ataulfo) variety. These smallish yellow-skinned specimens have minimal fiber and have beautiful deep orange flesh. Whichever kind of mango you have, it will continue to ripen after picking; at its peak, it will feel slightly soft and the skin may become slightly wrinkled.

**To dice a mango,** slice a bit off the stem end of the mango to create a stable base. Set the mango down on the cut end and slice down along one of the broad sides of the fruit. Try to cut as close to the large flat pit as possible; if you hit it with your knife, just reposition your knife slightly and continue on. Repeat on the other side. You should have two large cup-shaped pieces of skin-on fruit, plus the remaining pit. Take one of the cup-shaped pieces and use a paring knife to cut a crosshatch pattern into the flesh, being careful to avoid piercing the skin. Turn the cup inside out so that the fruit chunks splay out. Carefully trim the chunks away from the skin with the paring knife. Cut the two remaining strips of fruit away from the pit and trim off the skin. The pit makes for good nibbling, so don't let it go to waste.

## BANANAS

We don't use any special variety of bananas, but we do make sure they're organic, and we let them ripen fully before using them, especially if we're baking with them or using them in ice cream. The darker the bananas, the more sugar and flavor they have and the better they taste.

# TOASTED COCONUT ICE CREAM

Makes about 1 quart

We use two different types of toasted coconut in this ice cream: unsweetened coconut steeps with the milk and cream to impart a full coconut flavor without added sugar, and sweetened coconut is folded into the finished ice cream for just a bit of texture and crunch. We've found that using unsweetened coconut at the end doesn't give the ice cream the same delicate bite.

## AT A GLANCE

| TECHNIQUE: | SPECIAL EQUIPMENT: | INFUSING AND CHILLING TIME: | SHELF LIFE: |
|---|---|---|---|
| Ice cream (page 12) | Ice cream machine | 20 minutes, plus 2 hours or overnight | 1 week |

1 cup unsweetened dried shredded coconut

1/4 cup sweetened dried shredded coconut

2 cups heavy cream

1 1/4 cups 1% or 2% milk

3/4 cup sugar

1/4 teaspoon kosher salt

5 large egg yolks

### TOAST THE COCONUT

1. Position racks in the top and bottom thirds of the oven and preheat the oven to 350°F.

2. Spread the unsweetened coconut on a small rimmed baking sheet, and spread the sweetened coconut on another small rimmed baking sheet. Put them both in the oven and toast, stirring every 2 minutes, until golden brown, 4 to 6 minutes total.

   Alternatively, you can toast the coconut on the stove top in a dry skillet over medium heat. Toast the two types separately, and stir constantly to prevent burning. This is a faster and more energy-efficient method, but it requires constant attention and does not toast the coconut quite as evenly.

### INFUSE THE MILK/CREAM

3. In a heavy nonreactive saucepan, stir together the cream, milk, half of the sugar (6 tablespoons), and the salt.

4. Put the pan over medium-high heat. When the mixture just begins to bubble around the edges, stir in the unsweetened coconut. When slight bubbling resumes around the edges of the pan, remove from the heat and cover the pan. Let steep for 15 to 20 minutes, or until a distinct coconut flavor has infused into the liquid. (Taste it to monitor the progress.)

5. Strain through a fine-mesh strainer into a bowl, pressing on the coconut to extract as much liquid as possible. Rinse the pan, then return the infused cream to the saucepan.

### MAKE THE BASE

6. In a medium heatproof bowl, whisk the yolks just to break them up, then whisk in the remaining sugar (6 tablespoons). Set aside.

7. Uncover the cream mixture and put the pan over medium-high heat. When the mixture approaches a bare simmer, reduce the heat to medium.

8. Carefully scoop out about ½ cup of the hot cream mixture and, whisking the eggs constantly, add the cream to the bowl with the egg yolks. Repeat, adding another ½ cup of the hot cream to the bowl with the yolks. Using a heatproof rubber spatula, stir the cream in the saucepan as you slowly pour the egg-and-cream mixture from the bowl into the pan.

9. Cook the mixture carefully over medium heat, stirring constantly, until it is thickened, coats the back of a spatula, and holds a clear path when you run your finger across the spatula, 1 to 2 minutes longer.

10. Strain the base through a fine-mesh strainer into a clean container. Set the container into an ice-water bath, wash your spatula, and use it to stir the base occasionally until it is cool. Remove the container from the ice-water bath, cover with plastic wrap, and refrigerate the base for at least 2 hours or overnight.

## FREEZE THE ICE CREAM

11. Freeze in your ice cream machine according to the manufacturer's instructions. While the ice cream is churning, put the container you'll use to store the ice cream into the freezer. Add the sweetened coconut in the last minute or so of churning, or fold it in by hand after transferring the ice cream to the chilled container. Enjoy right away or, for a firmer ice cream, freeze for at least 4 hours.

# MANGO SAUCE

Makes about 2 ½ cups

This flavorful sauce adds a sweet-tart note and a hit of color to ice cream, cakes, and other desserts.

## AT A GLANCE ·······································································

SPECIAL EQUIPMENT: Blender or food processor

SHELF LIFE: 2 days

·································································································

2 large or 3 medium ripe mangoes, peeled, pitted, and cut into chunks

2 tablespoons strained fresh lime juice

⅛ teaspoon kosher salt

½ cup 1:1 Simple Syrup (page 18), cooled

1. Put the mangoes in a blender or food processor and purée until smooth. Strain through a fine-mesh strainer into a medium bowl, pressing on the solids to extract as much of the purée as possible. Stir in the lime juice and salt. Add ¼ cup simple syrup; taste and add more if needed. Chill before serving.

# CARAMELIZED BANANA ICE CREAM

Makes about 1 quart | Pictured on page 67

In order to bring out the most intense banana flavor possible, we cook very ripe bananas with brown sugar until they're caramelized and bubbly. This reduces the water content, intensifies the banana flavor, and brings out the sweetness of the fruit.

In this recipe especially, the riper your bananas, the better and more flavorful your ice cream will be. At the Creamery, we wait until they are almost black before using them! The optional rum gives the ice cream a real Bananas Foster-type flavor.

## AT A GLANCE

| TECHNIQUE: | SPECIAL EQUIPMENT: | CHILLING TIME: | SHELF LIFE: |
|---|---|---|---|
| Ice cream (page 12) | Ice cream machine | 2 hours or overnight | 1 week |

2 very ripe medium bananas, peeled

1/2 cup packed light or dark brown sugar

5 large egg yolks

1 3/4 cup heavy cream

3/4 cup 1% or 2% milk

1/4 teaspoon kosher salt

1 to 2 tablespoons dark rum (optional)

1 teaspoon pure vanilla extract

### CARAMELIZE THE BANANAS

1. Combine the bananas and brown sugar in medium skillet and use a fork to smoosh them together into a nearly liquid paste. Put the pan over medium heat and cook, stirring frequently, until the mixture is dark golden brown and slightly reduced, 5 to 7 minutes.

2. Let cool briefly, then purée in a blender or food processor to make a smooth paste. Set aside.

### MAKE THE BASE

3. In a medium heatproof bowl, whisk the yolks just to break them up. Set aside.

4. In a heavy nonreactive saucepan, stir together the cream, milk, and salt and put the pan over medium-high heat. When the mixture approaches a bare simmer, reduce the heat to medium.

5. Carefully scoop out about 1/2 cup of the hot cream mixture and, whisking the eggs constantly, add the cream to the bowl with the egg yolks. Repeat, adding another 1/2 cup of the hot cream to the bowl with the yolks. Using a heatproof rubber spatula, stir the cream in the saucepan as you slowly pour the egg-and-cream mixture from the bowl into the pan.

6. Cook the mixture carefully over medium heat, stirring constantly, until it is thickened, coats the back of a spatula, and holds a clear path when you run your finger across the spatula, 1 to 2 minutes longer.

7. Strain the base through a fine-mesh strainer into a clean container. Set the container into an ice-water bath, wash your spatula, and use it to stir the base occasionally until it is cool. Remove the container from the ice-water bath, cover with plastic wrap, and refrigerate the base for at least 2 hours or overnight.

## FREEZE THE ICE CREAM

8. Add the rum (if using) and vanilla extract to the base and stir until blended.

9. Freeze in your ice cream machine according to the manufacturer's instructions. While the ice cream is churning, put the container you'll use to store the ice cream into the freezer. Enjoy right away or, for a firmer ice cream, transfer to the chilled container and freeze for at least 4 hours.

**MAKE IT YOUR OWN**
* Add chopped toasted macadamia nuts (see page 114) and finely chopped bittersweet chocolate.

**SERVE IT WITH . . .**
* Salted Caramel Ice Cream (page 61) or Balsamic Strawberry Ice Cream (page 138)
* Caramel Sauce (page 71), Whipped Cream (page 51), and Brown Sugar Graham Crackers (page 66) to make our Afternoon Snack sundae

# CHOCOLATE COCONUT "ICE CREAM"

Makes about 1 quart

When we first opened our ice cream shop, our vegan (dairy-free) ice cream was made with soy milk and silken tofu. It was good, but not great, and it lacked the rich creaminess of our dairy-based ice creams. Then it occurred to us: coconut milk! It has plenty of fat for a creamy mouthfeel, and the coconut flavor is a terrific pairing for chocolate.

Don't be tempted to use "lite" coconut milk; the full amount of fat is essential for delicious results.

## AT A GLANCE

| TECHNIQUE: | SPECIAL EQUIPMENT: | CHILLING TIME: | SHELF LIFE: |
|---|---|---|---|
| Sorbet (page 17) | Ice cream machine | At least 1 hour or up to overnight | 1 week |

2 cans (13.5 ounces each) coconut milk

3/4 cup sugar

2 ounces (1/2 cup plus 1 tablespoon) cocoa powder, measured then sifted

1/4 cup tapioca syrup or corn syrup

1/2 teaspoon kosher salt

1/2 teaspoon pure vanilla extract

### MAKE THE BASE

1. Combine all of the ingredients in a blender or food processor and purée until blended and smooth.

2. Transfer to a container, cover, and refrigerate for at least 1 hour, or up to overnight.

### FREEZE THE ICE CREAM

3. Freeze in your ice cream machine according to the manufacturer's instructions, being careful not to overchurn. While the ice cream is churning, put the container you'll use to store the ice cream into the freezer. Enjoy right away or, for a firmer ice cream, transfer to the chilled container and freeze for about 4 hours.

---

**MAKE IT YOUR OWN**

❋ Add 1/2 cup each chopped almonds and diced marshmallows to make rocky road!

**SERVE IT WITH . . .**

❋ Toasted Coconut Ice Cream (page 200) or Caramelized Banana Ice Cream (page 202)

❋ Caramel Sauce (page 71) and chopped toasted almonds (see page 114)

---

# MANGO SORBET

Makes about 1 quart | Pictured on page 197

Fresh mangoes have a uniquely luscious texture that becomes very fine and smooth with purée-ing, which makes them particularly well suited to sorbet. The addition of a bit of tapioca syrup helps make the sorbet extra creamy when frozen.

## AT A GLANCE

| TECHNIQUE: | SPECIAL EQUIPMENT: | SHELF LIFE: |
|---|---|---|
| Sorbet (page 17) | Ice cream machine | 1 week |

3 large ripe mangoes (about 3 pounds total)
6 tablespoons water
6 tablespoons tapioca syrup or corn syrup
3 tablespoons strained fresh lime juice
$1/4$ teaspoon kosher salt
$1/2$ cup 1:1 Simple Syrup (page 18)

### MAKE THE BASE

1. Peel the mangoes, cut the flesh away from the pits, and cut the fruit into chunks (see page 199 for detailed instructions). Purée in a blender or food processor until smooth. Strain into a medium bowl, pressing on the solids to extract as much liquid as possible.

2. Add the water, tapioca syrup, lime juice, salt, and $1/2$ cup of the simple syrup to the strained purée. Whisk until well combined and the salt is completely dissolved.

3. Taste the base. It should taste just a bit too sweet (once the sorbet is frozen, it will lose some of its sweetness). Add the remaining simple syrup if you need it.

### FREEZE THE SORBET

4. Freeze in your ice cream machine according to the manufacturer's instructions. While the sorbet is churning, put the container you'll use to store the sorbet into the freezer. Enjoy right away or, for a firmer sorbet, transfer to the chilled container and freeze for about 4 hours.

---

**MAKE IT YOUR OWN**

❊ This recipe can easily be made with other fruit, such as nectarines (as shown on the cover). Use 3 pounds of nectarines (about 6 large nectarines), pitted and cut into chunks. Purée the fruit, then combine with the other ingredients as directed (no need to strain). Just use lemon juice instead of lime juice.

**SERVE IT WITH . . .**

❊ Toasted Coconut Ice Cream (page 200) or Crème Fraîche Ice Cream (page 38)

---

# PINEAPPLE-MINT ICE POPS

Makes nine 3-ounce ice pops | Pictured on page 20

The heady, sweet pineapple in these beautiful and refreshing pops is a perfect foil for the gentle brace of fresh mint.

## AT A GLANCE

| TECHNIQUE: | SPECIAL EQUIPMENT: | CHILLING TIME: | SHELF LIFE: |
|---|---|---|---|
| Ice pops (page 20) | Ice pop molds | At least 4 hours | 1 week |

1 large ripe pineapple (about 3½ pounds), peeled, cored, and cut into chunks

⅓ cup lightly packed coarsely chopped fresh mint leaves

½ cup 1:1 Simple Syrup (page 18), cooled

Juice of 1 small lime, strained

⅛ teaspoon salt

### MAKE THE BASE

1. In a food processor or blender, purée the pineapple and mint just until smooth. (Avoid processing any longer than necessary, as it will make the mixture too frothy.) Strain through a fine-mesh strainer into a medium bowl, pressing on the solids to extract as much juice as possible. Add half of the simple syrup, the lime juice, and salt and whisk to blend.

2. Taste the base. It should taste just a bit too sweet (once frozen, it will lose some of its sweetness). Add the remaining simple syrup if you need it.

### FREEZE THE ICE POPS

3. Transfer the base to a liquid measuring cup and pour into ice pop molds. Insert the sticks and freeze until completely solid, about 4 hours. Unmold just before serving.

> **MAKE IT YOUR OWN**
> ❊ Add 1 tablespoon light rum or tequila for an adults-only spin on a tropical cocktail! Don't be tempted to add more than 1 tablespoon, though, as it will prevent the pops from freezing properly.

# BANANAS BRÛLÉE

Makes 2 banana halves, for 1 banana split

These bananas are the secret to the best banana split you'll ever have. A propane or butane kitchen torch (the kind you'd use to make crème brûlée) is the best tool for the job. You can use your broiler instead, but the bananas will not caramelize nearly as evenly.

Use bananas that are ripe but not super soft; very ripe ones are too delicate and will fall apart when you move them. This is one recipe where conventional (not organic) sugar works best because organic sugar does not melt evenly and has a tendency to burn. Make these at the very last minute possible, as the caramelized sugar will start to dissolve and melt very quickly.

AT A GLANCE ·······················································································

SPECIAL EQUIPMENT: Brûlée torch                          SHELF LIFE: Use immediately

··············································································································

1 medium-ripe banana
1¹/₂ to 2 tablespoons sugar

1. Halve the banana lengthwise and peel off the skin. Place the banana halves cut side up on a flameproof surface such as a baking sheet set on a few layers of kitchen towels. Sprinkle the sugar evenly over the bananas and use the back of a spoon to smooth the sugar evenly over the surface.

2. Light your torch and wave it back and forth over the sugar. It's important to keep the flame in constant motion to avoid burned spots. Continue until the sugar is melted and caramelized.

3. Let cool for a few seconds to let the sugar harden, then use a spatula to transfer the bananas to a serving dish. Serve right away.

# COCONUT MACAROONS

Makes about 20 cookies

These cookies, which we make year-round, have many loyal fans at Bi-Rite Market and the Creamery alike. You can bake these cookies in the traditional mound shapes, or flatten them out for use in ice cream sandwiches.

In addition to being pretty and delicious, they're also a good option for those avoiding wheat.

AT A GLANCE ••••••••••••••••••••••••••••••••••••••••••••••••••••••••••••••••••••••••••••••

CHILLING TIME: At least 2 hours or up to overnight          SHELF LIFE: 1 week

••••••••••••••••••••••••••••••••••••••••••••••••••••••••••••••••••••••••••••••••••••••

1 cup sugar

1/2 cup egg whites (from about 4 large eggs)

2 tablespoons tapioca syrup or corn syrup

1 teaspoon pure vanilla extract

1/4 teaspoon kosher salt

3 cups (8 ounces) finely shredded unsweetened coconut (organic, if possible)

1. Put about 1/2 inch of water in the bottom of a double boiler or medium saucepan and bring to a simmer over medium-high heat.

2. In the top of the double boiler or in a medium nonreactive bowl, whisk together all of the ingredients except the coconut. Put the double boiler insert or bowl over but not touching the simmering water. Cook, whisking frequently, until the mixture becomes somewhat translucent but still has some visible granules of sugar (about 3/4 of the sugar should be dissolved), 2 to 3 minutes.

3. Remove from the heat and stir in the coconut. Cover the bowl with plastic wrap and chill until the dough is firm, at least 2 hours or up to overnight. (This is a very sticky dough even after it is chilled thoroughly, but it will firm up quite a bit in the refrigerator.)

4. When you're ready to bake, position racks in the top and bottom thirds of the oven and preheat the oven to 350°F. Line two baking sheets with parchment paper.

   Scoop up 2 tablespoons of dough and form it into a ball. Repeat until all the dough has been shaped. For traditionally shaped (mounded) macaroons, space the balls 2 inches apart on the baking sheets and leave them as is. For flat cookies that can be used for ice cream sandwiches, space the balls 3 inches apart and use water-dipped fingertips to flatten them until they are about 3 inches in diameter and 1/4 inch thick.

5. Bake for 10 minutes, and then rotate the baking sheets top to bottom and front to back. Continue to bake until the cookies are golden brown on top, about 5 minutes longer for flattened cookies and about 10 minutes longer for rounded cookies.

6. When the cookies come out of the oven, slide the sheet of parchment, cookies and all, onto a cooling rack. Let the cookies cool completely before peeling them off of the parchment (otherwise they will fall apart). Line the baking sheet with another sheet of parchment and bake any remaining dough.

Front left: Coconut Macaroons with Chocolate Ice Cream
(page 78); front right: Dark Chocolate Cookies (page 90)
with Balsamic Strawberry Ice Cream (page 138)

# SOURCES

## CHOCOLATE

**EL REY** Makers of our favorite white chocolate, as well as bittersweet and milk varieties. *chocolateselrey.com*

**MADÉCASSE** Makers of organic chocolate from Madagascar. *madecasse.com*

**VALRHONA** Excellent French chocolate; widely available. *valrhona-chocolate.com*

**DAGOBA** Organic chocolate for baking and eating. *dagobachocolate.com*

**CALLEBAUT** Makers of bittersweet, milk, and white chocolate; widely available. *callebaut.com*

## CITRUS OILS

**ETRURIA GOURMET** Makers of lemon oil, bergamot olive oil, and blood orange olive oil. *etruriagourmet.com*

**BOYAJIAN** Makers of lemon, orange, and lime oils. *boyajianinc.com*

## COFFEE AND TEA

**RITUAL ROASTERS** Definitely the best coffee in San Francisco—and perhaps in America! *ritualroasters.com*

**TEANCE** Our source for *matcha* tea powder as well as Earl Grey and other loose teas. *teance.com*

## HERBS AND SPICES

**FLAVORGANICS** Our source for peppermint extract. *flavorganics.com*

**THE GINGER PEOPLE** Makers of the ginger spread we use in our Brown Sugar Ice Cream with a Ginger-Caramel Swirl (page 63). *gingerpeople.com*

**SPICELY** High-quality organic dried herbs and spices; available at many Whole Foods locations. *spicely.com*

## VANILLA

**MADÉCASSE** Producers of vanilla beans and vanilla extract, as well as wonderful bean-to-bar chocolates. *madecasse.com*

**THE VANILLA.COMPANY** Another source for fair-trade vanilla beans and extract, in bulk quantities. *vanilla.com*

## OTHER HIGH-QUALITY AND HARD-TO-FIND INGREDIENTS

**THE BAKER'S CATALOGUE** Purveyors of just about every type of baking ingredient, tool, and equipment you might need. *kingarthurflour.com*

**JB PRINCE** Sellers of difficult-to-find pastry equipment. *jbprince.com*

**BRIESS** Makers of the tapioca syrup we use at Bi-Rite Creamery (sold in food-service sizes only). *briess.com*

**NATURE'S FLAVORS** Online source for tapioca syrup in home-sized quantities. *naturesflavors.com*

# ACKNOWLEDGMENTS

WE HAVE SO MANY PEOPLE to thank for helping to make this book a reality!

Thanks to our personable, friendly, and talented staff at Bi-Rite Creamery: the baking team, Debby, Matt, Natalie, Olivia, and Coral; ice cream makers Ezequiel and Luis; the Cream Team scoopers (that's what they call themselves!), Raul, Josh, Jacqi, Andrea, Daniel, Katie, Elisa, Priscilla, Mercedes, Surya, Laura, Emily, and Celina; the prep/dish boys, Selvin, Juan Carlos, Denis, Rodolfo, Tony, and Rudy; and the bakers' helpers, Javier and Trini.

Many thanks to Sam Mogannan and Calvin Tsay, our wonderful business partners, for their great advice and constant support.

Thanks are also due to the staff at our sister company, Bi-Rite Market, especially Liz Martinez, for all her knowledge and invaluable help; Simon Richard, for letting us know about the freshest and best-tasting produce; Kirsten Bourne, for her tireless marketing help; and Mary and John Thompson, for making sure our vendors and staff get paid on time. Thanks also to our mentors Patrick Delessio, Rodney Cerdan, and Shannan Hobbs.

If you own an ice cream shop, the best person to know is a refrigeration/freezer repair guy. Dave Cava, from Central Refrigeration, is our man! He is *always* willing to take a phone call from us and come to our rescue. We're also grateful to Steve Thompson at Emery Thompson and everyone at Straus Family Creamery, especially Albert Straus and Anna Kharbas.

We're grateful to our agent, Katherine Cowles, who helped us hone our idea and guide us through the writing and publishing process, and to the entire staff at Ten Speed, especially Aaron Wehner, Melissa Moore, Nancy Austin, Katy Brown, and Kristin Casemore.

To our neighbors along (and above) 18th Street, thank you for your patience and understanding!

Thanks to our photographer, Paige Green, for creating such gorgeous photographs, for being such a joy to work with, and knowing just what to say to make our kid models laugh and smile. Without Sachi Henrietta and Esther Feinman, who helped us with prop styling, we surely would have gone cross-eyed trying to pick surfaces and textiles for all our photos. Thanks also to Rae Dunn for generously lending us props from her collection.

Many, many thanks to our recipe testers, who were not afraid to tell us when our instructions didn't make sense. Your input and feedback helped us step outside the commercial kitchen and into the mind of the home cook. On behalf of all of our readers, thank you to Kathleen Bradley, Martha Cheng, James Cribb, Dan Duane, Blake Engel, Rachel and Pete Hartsough, Erin Kuka, Brett Lider, Jean Lider, Miranda Martin, Dave McElroy, Dina Rao, Sue Simon, and Michelle Warner.

### FROM KRIS

I would not be where I am today without Anne and Sam. Thank you to Anne for knowing how to make me laugh when I don't want to, for being an incredible mentor, and most of all for being a wonderful friend and business partner. Thank you to Sam for believing in me and thinking of me as more than just an employee.

Thank you to Calvin, our business partner who always asks the hard questions and is the best listener.

To my husband Nate, who (if I let him) would eat sweets for breakfast, lunch, and dinner. Thank you for being you and making the *occasional* cocktail when needed!

Thank you to my mom and dad, who have always taught me that hard work will pay off and have always belived in my eccentricities.

Thank you to Dabney, the glue that holds it all together. This book has been so much fun to work on with you; I can't wait for the next one!

And heap-loads of thanks to the Creamery staff, my other family. You guys are the best, each and every one of you.

### FROM ANNE

Thank you to my husband Sam and our daughters Zoe and Olive for their constant support and love. Sam, you are always there when I need a sounding board and another set of eyes.

Thank you to my wonderful business partner Kris for journeying with me through so many amazing adventures in the past ten (plus) years. This book has been a great experience and so much fun to work on with you.

Thank you to Dabney for keeping us on track and organized with our weekly phone meetings and spreadsheets. You are fantastic to work with. I only wish you were closer.

Thank you to my mother, for inspiring me to bake.

### FROM DABNEY

My name would not appear on this book without the enthusiasm and open-mindedness of Anne Walker and Kris Hoogerhyde, who did not seem to mind that I worked on this book in various far-flung locations, none of which happened to be San Francisco. I'm so honored to work on this project with you two incredibly talented ladies.

Thanks to Tyler, who, despite not being able to eat sweets, willingly gave up our entire freezer for months on end while I filled it with endless quarts of ice cream. And thanks to all of my Honolulu friends who not only took all that ice cream off of my hands, but also contributed empty quart containers to the cause. I may never know if you only liked me for my ice cream, but considering how fun and entertaining you all are, it doesn't really matter to me!

# MEASUREMENT CONVERSION CHARTS

| VOLUME | | |
|---|---|---|
| **U.S.** | **Imperial** | **Metric** |
| 1 tablespoon | 1/2 fl oz | 15 ml |
| 2 tablespoons | 1 fl oz | 30 ml |
| 1/4 cup | 2 fl oz | 60 ml |
| 1/3 cup | 3 fl oz | 90 ml |
| 1/2 cup | 4 fl oz | 120 ml |
| 2/3 cup | 5 fl oz (1/4 pint) | 150 ml |
| 3/4 cup | 6 fl oz | 180 ml |
| 1 cup | 8 fl oz (1/3 pint) | 240 ml |
| 1 1/4 cups | 10 fl oz (1/2 pint) | 300 ml |
| 2 cups (1 pint) | 16 fl oz (2/3 pint) | 480 ml |
| 2 1/2 cups | 20 fl oz (1 pint) | 600 ml |
| 1 quart | 32 fl oz (1 2/3 pints) | 1 l |

| TEMPERATURE | |
|---|---|
| **Fahrenheit** | **Celsius/Gas Mark** |
| 250°F | 120°C/gas mark 1/2 |
| 275°F | 135°C/gas mark 1 |
| 300°F | 150°C/gas mark 2 |
| 325°F | 160°C/gas mark 3 |
| 350°F | 180 or 175°C/gas mark 4 |
| 375°F | 190°C/gas mark 5 |
| 400°F | 200°C/gas mark 6 |
| 425°F | 220°C/gas mark 7 |
| 450°F | 230°C/gas mark 8 |
| 475°F | 245°C/gas mark 9 |
| 500°F | 260°C |

| LENGTH | |
|---|---|
| **Inch** | **Metric** |
| 1/4 inch | 6 mm |
| 1/2 inch | 1.25 cm |
| 3/4 inch | 2 cm |
| 1 inch | 2.5 cm |
| 6 inches (1/2 foot) | 15 cm |
| 12 inches (1 foot) | 30 cm |

| WEIGHT | |
|---|---|
| **U.S./Imperial** | **Metric** |
| 1/2 oz | 15 g |
| 1 oz | 30 g |
| 2 oz | 60 g |
| 1/4 lb | 115 g |
| 1/3 lb | 150 g |
| 1/2 lb | 225 g |
| 3/4 lb | 350 g |
| 1 lb | 450 g |

# INDEX

**SWEET CREAM** *and* **SUGAR CONES**

Published in the United States by Ten Speed Press, an
imprint of the Crown Publishing Group, a division of
Random House, Inc., New York.
www.crownpublishing.com
www.tenspeed.com

Ten Speed Press and the Ten Speed Press colophon are
registered trademarks of Random House, Inc.

Library of Congress Cataloging-in-Publication Data is
on file with the publisher

ISBN 978-1-60774-184-8
eISBN 978-1-60774-185-5

Printed in China

Design by Katy Brown and Nancy Austin

10 9 8 7 6 5 4 3 2 1

First Edition